MW00453730

Warrior • 49

Landsknecht Soldier 1486–1560

John Richards • Illustrated by Gerry Embleton

First published in Great Britain in 2002 by Osprey Publishing,
Midland House, West Way, Botley, Oxford OX2 0PH, UK
44-02 23rd St, Suite 219, Long Island City, NY 11101, USA
E-mail: info@ospreypublishing.com

© 2002 Osprey Publishing Ltd.

All rights reserved. Apart from any fair dealing for the purpose of private study, research,
criticism or review, as permitted under the Copyright, Designs and Patents Act, 1988,
no part of this publication may be reproduced, stored in a retrieval system, or transmitted
in any form or by any means, electronic, electrical, chemical, mechanical, optical,
photocopying, recording or otherwise, without the prior written permission of the
copyright owner. Enquiries should be addressed to the Publishers.

Transferred to digital print on demand 2009

First published 2002
3rd impression 2007

Printed and bound by Cadmus Communications, USA

A CIP catalogue record for this book is available from the British Library

ISBN: 978 1 84176 243 2

Editorial by Thomas Lowres
Design by Ken Vail Graphic Design, Cambridge, UK
Index by Alan Rutter
Originated by Magnet Harlequin, Uxbridge, UK
Typeset in Helvetica Neue and ITC New Baskerville.

Dedication
To my daughter Phoebe, my little shining light.

Artist's Note
Readers may care to note that the original paintings from which the colour plates in this book were prepared are available for private
sale. All reproduction copyright whatsoever is retained by the Publishers. More information can be found at www.gerryembleton.com
The Publishers regret that they can enter into no correpondence upon this matter.

Acknowledgements
Gerry Embleton for sharing the research and many a laugh. On to the next Saubannerzug!
Frau A. Blaha, Oberarchivrätin, Thüringisches Hauptstaatsarchiv Weimar, for helping so much in the search for photographs of the diary
of Paul von Dolstein (ThHStAW. Ernestinisches Gesamtarchiv, Reg. S fol.460, Nr. 6BL. 1r-13r).
John Howe and Nicholas Michael for sharing a passionate interest.
Eli Tanner for his invaluable help.
The two gentlemen who as usual opened their extensive private collections to me.
Annette Richards for scanning the illustrations and organising the manuscript.
Anne Embleton-Perret for her translations.
Helen Bosshard for keeping the modern Landsknechts off my back while writing the book.
Thanks to everyone who shares my peculiar passions and has helped directly and indirectly with this book.
To the ghosts of Urs Graf, Niklaus Manuel Deutsch, Paul Dolnstein and Paul Guldi, who in fact started this book 500 years ago.

FOR A CATALOGUE OF ALL BOOKS PUBLISHED BY OSPREY
MILITARY AND AVIATION PLEASE CONTACT:

Osprey Direct, c/o Random House Distribution Center,
400 Hahn Road, Westminster, MD 21157
Email: uscustomerservice@ospreypublishing.com

Osprey Direct, The Book Service Ltd, Distribution Centre,
Colchester Road, Frating Green, Colchester, Essex, CO7 7DW
E-mail: customerservice@ospreypublishing.com

www.ospreypublishing.com

CONTENTS

LANDSKNECHT SOLDIER 1486–1560

INTRODUCTION

To understand the importance of the Landsknechts in the evolution of modern warfare, it is of great interest to the military historian to examine the creation of this force and the developments in tactics at this watershed in European military history.

The previous century had shown the obsolescence of feudal armies. Lessons learned during battles fought at the end of the 15th century were to have a marked effect on the creation of the Landsknecht organisation. In fact, it is fair to say that the Burgundian Wars (1476–77) were the crucible in which the military tactics of the next four centuries were forged. The armies of Charles the Bold of Burgundy, an avid student of Roman tactics, were organised in the first truly modern way, instantly recognisable to today's soldier.

According to Frédéric de Gingins-la-Sarraz, the reorganisation of the Duke's army, carried out in Lausanne in May 1476 after the defeat at

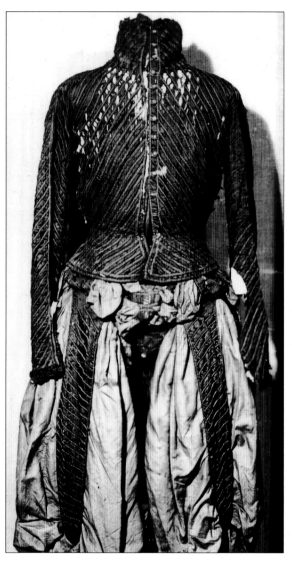

Pluderhosen. Although much loved by 19th-century and modern artists, they were not worn until the second half of the 16th century, when at times they appear to have been very popular. Above, an extremely rare surviving example, the costume of Erik Sture, worn at the time of his murder in 1567 and now preserved in Uppsala Cathedral, Sweden. On the left, an engraving, c.1560 caricatures a costume that was considered outlandish even at the time, but not by everyone! Two of this gentleman's admirers fight over him.
(Armemuseum, Stockholm (above) and Eli Tanner (left))

Grandson, showed four army corps, each commanded by a *chef superièure*, and each divided into two lines of battle. Each line of battle consisted of one company, each carrying the name of its individual captain and consisting of a mixture of squadrons of elite cavalry (*gens d'armes*, or men-at-arms), foot soldiers and archers, each unit commanded by a lieutenant. This army, supported by a strong artillery, was made up mainly of the remnants of the feudal system, namely armoured noblemen, and mercenary and levied foot soldiers and archers. As such, it probably lacked the cohesion and crucial esprit de corps of its far lesswell-organised opponent, the army of the Helvetic Confederation.

The cantons that made up the Helvetic Confederation had formed a defensive coalition at the end of the 13th century and over time various city states and other cantons in the area now known as Switzerland had joined this coalition. These were violent times and it was never difficult to recruit men with, if not true battle experience, then certainly a great deal of experience in the skirmishes that came with constant territorial and other disputes. In fact, the love of fighting, coupled with a spirit of adventure and the inevitable boredom of everyday country and city life, meant that the young men of this region would often form a *saubannerzug* (quite literally a hooligan band under the banner of a pig or boot) to raid neighbours or anybody that had incurred the wrath of a section of the populace at any given time. Wintertime (when there was least to do in the countryside) and public holidays (when the apprentices were free) were particularly prone to this type of public disorder. Constant training in the use of the pike, the halbard, the short sword and the dagger was therefore vital for survival in these times, and in times of crisis the Confederation could muster a well-trained and aggressive army with such ease that men would often have to be turned away.

Although the individuals were capable enough, the makeshift Confederate armies of which they formed a part were far less well organised. Individual units from a city state or canton would be led by a known personality of the region, such as the *schultheiss*, a nobleman from the local government or a leading personality who had distinguished himself in previous campaigns. These units would then be integrated to form an army of three main sections, the *vorhut* (van), *gewalthaufen* (centre) and *nachhut* (rear), with each individual unit vying for the honour of being at the front. Once the individual units had been formed into large pike blocks, with crossbow and handgun support, the constant training with the pike paid off and these huge formations of some 10,000 men were as well drilled as any unit in history and could be manoeuvred with a simple, minimum set of (probably standardised) commands. As history records, the cohesiveness of the Confederates (aggressive, well-trained individuals fighting alongside their friends, families and neighbours) beat the far better organised and equipped, but far less motivated army of Charles the Bold at Grandson, Murten and Nancy and led directly to the death of Charles and the fall of Burgundy as a major power in Europe.

Veteran Halbardier. This grizzled warrior appears in full plumage, hung about with the gold chains that represent his portable fortune. (Eli Tanner)

THE ORIGINS OF THE LANDSKNECHTS

The overwhelming defeat of a major power such as Burgundy led to a good deal of attention being paid to the Confederate way of waging war. Maximilian I, heir to the throne of the Holy Roman Empire, who had married the daughter of Charles the Bold and inherited Burgundy after Charles's death at Nancy (1477), would certainly have been caught up in these events and was subsequently greatly influenced by the Confederate victories. When called upon to defend his inheritance against France, he was able to raise an army of Flemish foot soldiers, which, in Confederate style, was to beat the French army of men-at-arms, archers and crossbowmen at Guinegate (7 August 1479). Unfortunately, like the Confederate armies before them, Maximilian's army of levied citizens disappeared into thin air once the fighting was over, and he soon realised that a more structured, permanent force was needed if he was to succeed in defending his valuable inheritances against rebellions both outside and in.

It must be remembered that Maximilian was defending the territories of the Holy Roman Empire from France in the west, the Turks in the east, and at the same time trying to quell a host of smaller areas of unrest, from Sweden to Italy. He needed a reliable source of men for his armies, and he needed them quickly. Unlike the countries of the north, with low population density but high agricultural production, the lands of southern Germany and the Helvetic Confederation produced an inexhaustible supply of young men, eager for action, excitement and booty. Having seen with his own eyes the superiority of well-drilled foot formations against cavalry, he set about recruiting various armies from the thousands of mercenaries that flocked to his service, from

Mounted Crossbowmen and Light Horse, by Paul Dolstein, c.1500. There is nothing to show that these are friends or enemies. Dolstein has drawn the sort of light horse that fought in large numbers with and against the Landsknecht regiments. The details are meticulously drawn and corroborated by other artists of the time. (Thür. Hauptstaatsarchiv, Weimar)

the Rhine area, Alsace, Upper Germany, the Helvetic Confederation, the Low Countries and even Scotland. Initially the units raised were of dubious quality, but by 1486, the year in which he was voted King of Germany, he had already assembled two such armies of 3–4,000 men each. With the help of Confederate instructors, these armies of pikemen were turned into potent fighting forces.

The first documented mention of the Landsknechts (Landsknecht means servant of the country) was in 1486, when the council of the Helvetic Confederation was dealing with a diatribe by Konrad Gächuff, who had dared to suggest that, 'he would prefer to arm and train the Swabian or other Landsknecht, because one of them is worth two of us'. In 1487 Maximilian's commander, Graf Eitelfritz von Hohenzollern, was training these first units of Landsknechts in the streets of Bruges. By 1488 the 'Black Guard', formed in Friesland, apparently by Maximilian to defend his Low Country possessions, could almost be described as 'elite', doing sterling (if somewhat brutal) service for nearly 12 years in the territories around the North Sea, and in Sweden and in Denmark, before their total defeat at the hands of the Dithmarsch peasant army at Hemmingstedt (17 February 1500). In 1490 Maximilian was able to raise a strong Landsknecht force for the Hungarian Wars; but having regained his inherited territories to the east and successfully stormed the fortress of Stuhlweissenburg in Bohemia, his Landsknecht army promptly refused to continue the march on Budapest because of lack of pay and turned homewards, heavily laden with booty.

During this transition period between the Middle Ages and the 'New Age' of the Renaissance, Maximilian, brought up in the lore of the

Landsknechts c.1515–20, woodcut by George Lemberger (left), anonymous woodcut (right). Around 1515 and not so much before or after, there was a vogue among Landsknechts for appearing really ragged and outlandish. The soldiers depicted in the original paintings for the 'Triumph of Maximilian' wear their hose torn or rolled down, with the lining of their clothes hanging in tatters (16th-century 'punk' fashion!). (Eli Tanner (left), private collection (right))

medieval knight but convinced by the successes of the 'modern' foot soldier armies, realised that in order to prevent a re-occurrence of the events of Stuhlweissenburg he had to convert the colourful but unreliable mixture of mercenaries from all over Europe into a more unified, mainly Germanic and therefore more cohesive new military order, based on the organisation of the armies of Charles the Bold, the discipline of the religious military orders of medieval knights and the strike power of the pike formations of the Helvetic Confederation. Although his foreign policy was not always successful, his skill as an army reformer was undoubted, and he was to rediscover what the Romans had known centuries before and the Helvetic Confederation had again proven against Burgundy, namely the superiority of massed foot formations on the battlefield. With the rise of the Landsknechts, the monopoly of the Helvetic *Reisläufer* (Confederate mercenary) on the mercenary market was broken and an intense rivalry ensued. The characteristic structure of the Landsknecht armies, with their well-defined hierarchy and unusually high number of functionaries taking care of the myriad details of regimental organisation, each with a proper rank, rate of pay and position in the wider scheme, was to set the foundations of army structure for centuries to come.

ORGANISATION

The armies of Maximilian's father-in-law, Charles the Bold, had been extremely well organised, with a strict military hierarchy and an excellent logistics system, perfect for maintaining a semi-permanent standing army. They had failed because they lacked the decisive weapon of their Confederate enemies – a highly motivated massed foot formation. Having understood this lesson, Maximilian set about creating his new military order, recruiting an elite based on fighting prowess rather than birth and origin, and was responsible for introducing ritualised foot combat into the tournament for his knights. He himself always set the example, wearing the armour and weaponry of the foot soldier and taking his place in the ranks. On important occasions he would march with shouldered pike in the front rank of the Gewalthaufen, for example during the triumphant entry into Ghent (7 July 1485) or in front of Milan in 1516. Similarly, in 1505, Pfalzgraf Friedrich led a worthy group of princes and noblemen to the aid of his childhood friend, Archduke Philipp, the Emperor's son, at Arnhem. His whole group, armed in Landsknecht fashion with pikes and short sword, having arrived in Emmerich by ship and hearing that Philipp had given up his attack against the Count of Gelderland, shouldered their pikes and returned home on foot. Arriving in Xanten, they received the news that the Emperor would arrive there shortly. Embarrassed to be seen in such unbecoming attire, they swiftly handed their pikes to their servants. No sooner had the Emperor heard of this than he sent a message begging them to continue on their way without shame. He arrived in their midst ten days later and joined the march. The sight of Maximilian, arriving triumphantly in Cologne, marching pike-on-shoulder at the head of 900 lords and gentlemen, including two Rhine counts Palatine (Pfalzgrafen), two Saxon dukes, both Brandenburg

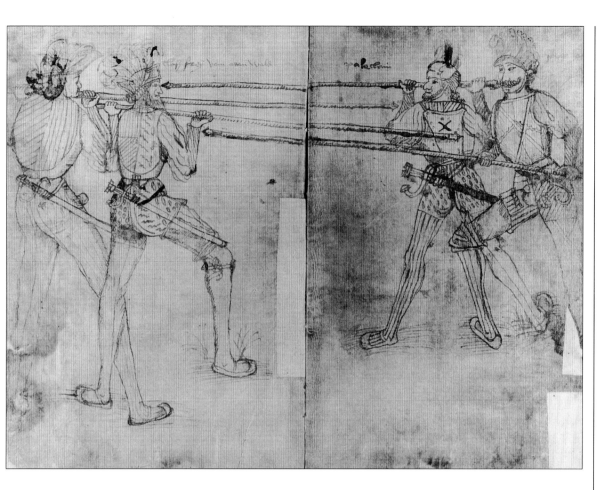

Pikemen, by Paul Dolstein, c.1500. These 4 pikeman in military pose appear to be more Dolstein's comrades. One, second from left, is Clas Frey von Attenwald, but the names of the others are illegible. (Thür. Hauptstaatsarchiv, Weimar)

Margraves (*Markgrafen*), the Dukes of Mecklenburg, Braunschweig and Würtemburg, and the nobleman Georg von Frundsberg, must have convinced much of the nobility to climb down off their high horses and train in the use of pike, halbard and short sword, thereby creating an invaluable pool of future officers for his Landsknecht units or *doppelsöldner* for his front ranks. With those of high birth standing shoulder to shoulder with those of more lowly origins, Maximilian was thus able to engender that elusive esprit de corps characteristic of the Confederate armies, where shared experiences and hardships made brothers-in-arms of otherwise quite disparate men.

RECRUITMENT

A relative standardised system was used all over Europe for the recruitment of mercenaries during this period. A warlord interested in recruiting mercenaries from a particular region would usually engage a known, experienced soldier to recruit a given number of men. A 'patent' or *bestallungbrief* (letter of appointment) would be prepared, naming the colonel (*obrist*) and laying down the size of the regiment and its structure, the amount of pay, the terms (articles of war) that applied and period of service (usually three to six months). Because Emperor Maximilian, his successor Charles V and the many princes that acted as

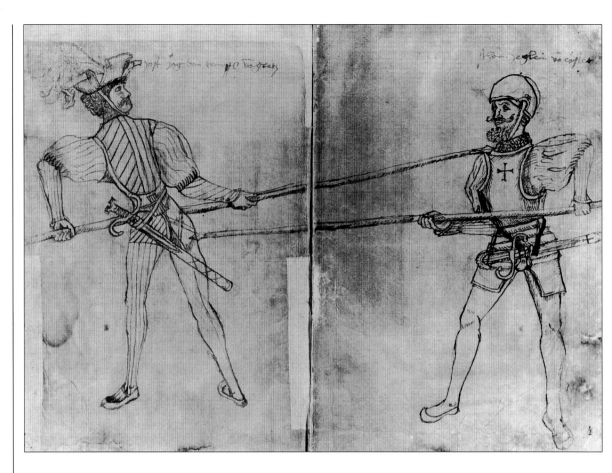

Landsknechts at Pike Practice, by Paul Dolstein, c.1500. Sadly we cannot read the names of Dolstein's two comrades depicted here. The young soldier on the left seems to be wearing his best clothes; the older, more experienced-looking soldier on the right is armed for war. (Thür. Hauptstaatsarchiv, Weimar)

warlords were often chronically short of cash, it was vital that the obrist was a man of great personal charisma, with the ability to recruit the maximum number of men in the shortest possible time, thus avoiding unnecessary expense. In fact, it could almost be said that the prime role of the colonel was to ensure that his troops were paid on a regular basis. He achieved this by careful management of the funds received from the warlord, either by raising bank loans or by bridging the gaps between pay days out of his own pocket. In view of the potentially disastrous consequences of a delay in pay, a combination of military prowess, a good head for business and considerable personal means were all desirable qualities. His importance was reflected in his pay, usually 100 times the monthly rate of the normal Landsknecht (four guilders), and by the time his personal train of wagons and horses were included, this could rise to 150 times the standard rate.

In most cases, the colonel was the senior officer; the only exceptions to this were in the case of a very large army, consisting of several regiments commanded by a *generalobrist*, or an army containing artillery and cavalry as well as the infantry, which would be commanded by a *feldobrist* (field colonel) or even a *generalfeldobrist* (for example Maximilian or one of his retinue). The colonel was entitled to a personal staff (the Imperial Diet of Worms in 1507 laid down an official entitlement of 22 men, but the actual number would depend on the personal wealth of the colonel), typically consisting of a chaplain, scribe, doctor, scout, personal quartermaster (to hunt out suitable lodgings),

The Recruitment, by Urs Graf, 1521. It is rare for a soldier-artist to record so effectively an important moment in his life. In May 1521 Francis I, King of France, signed an alliance with the Helvetic Confederacy. The Confederacy would supply troops for his forthcoming war in Italy. In June or July the young silversmith Urs Graf from Basel drew this poignant sketch showing a Reisläufer surrounded by the other players in the mercenary game. On the right, a Confederate innkeeper and his wife offer wine to their seated guests. A French recruiting officer, recognisable by the fleur-de-lys badge on his sleeve, reaches into his purse while a fool behind him laughs mockingly. Seated opposite, a stradiot and a cleric argue, while to their left, a peasant stares into a dark future. A moustachioed Landsknecht waits impatiently for his drink. Grim Death, as ever, listens and waits. Shortly after drawing this sketch, Urs Graf left Basel on 24 August with the company of Captain Antoni Dichtler for Milan and war. (Öffentliche Kunstsammlung, Basel)

interpreter, cook, *pfenningmeister* (penny master, to watch over regimental funds), an ensign for the regimental flag, a selection of drummers and fifers, as well as a bodyguard (*trabanten*) from his own household. The colonel also had a free hand over who should fill the important posts in the regiment, and he would invariably select these regimental officers from his friends in the nobility and wealthy citizenry. Originally, the term 'regiment' meant the entire force over which the colonel had absolute authority, but by 1550 the term became a proper unit of administration, meaning a force of anything up to ten *fahnlein* (approximately 3,000–5,000 men). These regimental officers were men with authority over the whole force and consisted of the second-in-command, a *locumtenens* or lieutenant-colonel, as well as the provost, responsible for upholding discipline in the regiment, the *schultheiss*, responsible for the application of law under the articles of war, the *oberster feldweibel*, responsible for the order of battle, and the *hurenweibel*, or 'whores' sergeant', responsible for organising the train.

Having chosen the officers, the colonel would set about choosing the captains for his individual *fähnlein*. 'Fähnlein' is the German word for a small banner and was the term given to the smallest administrative unit in the Landsknecht era. Typically a captain would be sent to a meeting point of a locality well known to him and would set about beating the *werbepatent* (recruiting patent) with the help of drums and fifes. Thus he would recruit approximately 300 to 500 men from a given area or town and this unit would consist of handgunners, pikemen and doppelsöldner, the mix and number depending on the funds available. It is important to understand that the men thus recruited were by no means 'a motley crew of journeymen, peasants and students'. In this

Landsknecht captain and bodyguard. This officer wears three-quarter armour imitating his slashed clothing. He wears a broad-brimmed plumed hat over a slashed coif, and his square-cut beard gives him a suitably fierce aspect. He wears his deep mail collar (bishop's mantel) under his breast and back plate so that it forms short 'sleeves' to cover his shoulders. Note the comfortable way his halbardier trabanten carries his halbards on their march. (private collection)

period, the strict guild laws meant that many apprentices were unable to take their master's examination and obtain their own workshops. Also, the population explosion and the large families of the day meant that there were plenty of 'third' sons, even in the wealthiest families, unable to enter the economic system in any useful way. The chance of adventure, pay and booty was therefore most attractive, and the men would flock to the banner 'like flies in the summer, so that the observer would wonder himself to death, where such a swarm had come from and where it had lain all winter'.

The standard Landsknecht pay (*sold*) of four guilders per month also compared favourably with that of civilian occupations (a typical building worker in the city [bricklayer, stonemason] would earn 2.5 guilders, a labourer 1.6 guilders per month) in 1515. The poor were immediately weeded out, as each soldier had to supply his own stout clothing, weapons and equipment, of a total value of about 12–14 guilders. A strict selection based on physical fitness, equipment and social and economic status, therefore meant that only the very best men were picked. In a period when an entire foot armour cost 16 guilders, an arquebus 3.5, a pike one and a charger (war horse) 44, only the sons of the gentry or those who already had enjoyed the fortunes of war could afford the best equipment. Men with the high level of armoured protection suitable for fighting in the front ranks, or men who could afford the arquebus and ancillary equipment of the elite handgunner units, were recruited as doppelsöldner, or double-pay soldiers, and received 8 guilders per month.

ARMY LIFE

The new recruit, having heard the drum and the reading of the patent, would step in front of the recruiting officer and give his name and place of birth, his age and his occupation. Having made sure that the new man understood the conditions of recruitment, the recruitment officer would then lay a coin 'on the gun barrel' and give instructions for the recruit to appear later in the month at a predetermined place of muster.

Once the agreed quota for a particular fähnlein was reached, the lengthy lists of recruits would be sent to the place of muster and added to the rest of the regiment. On the day of muster, the recruits would arrive from their respective areas and form up in the fähnleins they had elected to join. The mustering officer would appear together with the representatives of the regiment's legal system and the muster scribe. Now a portal would be set in front of the mustering officer through which each new recruit, once his name had been called, had to pass. Watched by the colonel on his horse and the captain of the respective fähnlein, the recruits would pass one by one in front of the officers, while the mustering officer called out the state of the equipment and the corresponding level of pay and the muster scribe made notes. Corruption was rife, and great care was taken to weed out the sick and the lame, the *doppelgängers* (literally 'double-walkers', recruits who passed twice through the portal) and those wearing armour and equipment borrowed from those who had passed before. Having passed the portal, the new recruit would then receive his docket with his rate of pay and walk to the pfennigmeister to receive his first *sold*.

THE ARTICLES OF WAR

Formalities over, the new recruit would now rejoin his fähnlein, and the regiment would form a circle around the colonel in order to hear the articles of war. These documents contained a list of the senior officers, the military and judicial codes, and the conditions of pay. As several copies were prepared, and one copy retained in the archives of the warlord, many have survived to the present day. Forerunners of the far stricter articles of later centuries, they were essentially a distillation of civilian/military behaviour and morals of the period, and the new recruit would certainly have felt comfortable with them. Essentially they specified that:

> those who flee in front of the enemy should be struck down by his comrades, those who desert will be considered without honour and will suffer punishment to body and life. No one is to burn and pillage without an order. Women and children, old people, priests and their churches are to be protected. No one should take anything in a friendly territory without paying for it. No one should hold a meeting without the permission of the Colonel. Mutinous soldiers should be reported immediately to an officer. Soldiers are not to assume that they are released from their duties should pay be delayed for any reason [the usual maximum acceptable delay was two weeks, but in practice this was pretty vague]. In the camp, comradeship is the order of the day. The sins of gambling and drinking are to be kept within reasonable limits. Any one who does not intervene in a fight immediately is considered guilty of fighting himself. Any one, having given suitable warning, who strikes down someone causing unrest, will not be punished. The Lord's name is not to be taken in vain. Soldiers should attend church regularly.

Landsknecht officer and escort, woodcut by Necker, 1520–30. This mounted officer with baton is certainly a colonel or higher, and is guarded by his two sturdy *trabanten* (bodyguards). 'Trabant' in modern terminology means satellite, a body like a moon that is constantly in orbit around a large object such as a planet and permanently tethered to it. The officer has the latest wheel-lock carbine hanging from his saddle and carries a baton marking his high rank. Following him are three mounted escorts, one lancer and two mounted crossbowmen. One has a crossbow bolt tucked into the slashed breast of his gown. All three wear fluted Maximilian-style armour under their gowns. (private collection)

The articles would invariably end with the statement that anyone who disobeyed these laws and the orders given by the officers would be considered oath breakers and would suffer punishment to life and limb.

Having the heard the articles of war, the entire regiment would now swear a formal oath, to abide by the same, and to 'serve the Emperor well and obey the officers without discussion or delay'. The schultheiss was the officer responsible for this part of the proceedings because all legal matters came under his jurisdiction. The oath was a vital component in maintaining discipline in these religious times. Generally once the oath was taken, the Warlord had nothing to fear and often much to gain from his troops until the perceived breach of contract in the form of a delay in pay led to mercenaries feeling justified in suspending service.

OFFICERS

The term 'officer' is used loosely here, as an officer corps did not yet exist and the term only starts to appear in German literature at the end of the 16th century. The posts in the regiment were generally known as *officium* and their holders *officiarius*. The officers that played a vital role in the life of a new recruit were determined during the muster and introduced to the assembled troops. In a period where there was no formal insignia of rank (apart form the flamboyance of dress), this introduction enabled the troops to recognise the various important figures and thus cemented the hierarchy. Apart from the schultheiss and the provost, whom the new recruit probably would have done well to avoid as much as possible, the following officers played a vital role in the wellbeing of the regiment. Their roles were so important in avoiding discontent among the soldiers that they received the same pay as the captains of the individual fähnleins (ten times the standard pay).

The *quartiermeister* (quartermaster) would ride ahead of the army and seek out lodging in towns or villages or find a suitable area for pitching the camp. A wrong decision in quartering 5,000 men could lead to flooded accommodation, mosquito-bitten soldiers, hours of back-breaking toil driving in pegs and building defences, and plenty of grumbling. The *proviantmeister* (master of provisions) had to be another capable businessman, as it is well known that an army marches on its stomach. Good fresh food would mean a healthy, content regiment, while the opposite could swiftly lead to mutiny and disaster. This was particularly important while the regiment was in friendly territory, as each Landsknecht was expected to pay for his own provisions. Careful negotiation with local businessmen won the hearts and minds of the local populace while ensuring for the soldiers a fair deal. With the basic needs of the

Feldarzt and assistants, c.1535. Note the large purse-like doctor's bag, the brass bowl and sponge, ointment pots and the leather case of surgical instruments being unpacked by this field doctor's assistant. Top left, the doctor examines a patient with a serious head wound, for which little could be done. (TMAG)

Schuldthos.

Im feldt man mich den Schulthos nent
Vnder der Lantzknecht regiment
Wo man im feldt helt ein gericht
So palt klag vnd antwurt geschicht
Red vnd wider red wirt gehört
So beschleuß ich dañ an dem ort
So es aber den todt drifft an
Vrteil ich biß auff den gemeinen man

Feldgerichts-Schultheiss (military judge and wife), woodcut by Hans Guldenmund the Elder, 1530. This couple's rich clothing is indicative of their exalted position within the regiment. (J.R.)

regiment taken care of, the *wachtmeister* (master of the watch) could ensure that the camp and the train were suitably guarded and fortified. The *feldarzt* (field doctor) was there to supervise the doctors in each of the fähnlein, to operate on wounds and attempt to avoid epidemics. While the treatment of wounds was very advanced in this period (soldiers often survived quite horrific wounds), the treatment of infection was not, and more men were lost to disease than to wounds sustained in battle. The *pfennigmeister* (master of the pennies) was responsible for the regular payment of *sold* and managed the financial transactions of the regiment. With monthly outgoings of 25,000 to 35,000 guilders for the average regiment (in the order of £8–10 million in today's money), this post carried considerable responsibility, and the pfennigmeister would be supported by a large staff of scribes.

The schultheiss, as mentioned above, was responsible for all legal matters regarding the regiment and would lead the schultheiss court. In a period where there was great distrust of 'Roman' judicial law and the incredibly complex judicial system (as well as a hatred of career lawyers), is was important that the schultheiss was not an academic from the civilian judicial system but a 'clever, practical man, well-versed in the law of war'.

The most interesting character in any Landsknecht army was without doubt the provost. Flamboyantly dressed, he was responsible for 'policing' the army, and his role was vital for morale. He 'has to know at all times what he should do and what he should leave. If he does too little, there is much disorder, disobedience and uproar in the camp. If he is too strict, there is much complaint, unhappiness, rioting and even mutiny. In all things he should be brave and serious, not sloppy and careless. Thus authority and respect will be his, while only the wrongdoers will fear him.'

A Landsknecht army that had been regularly paid was a good place to do business, and whenever the regiment was stationary for any period of time market traders arrived with wooden 'transport' barrels on their backs. Contemporary illustrations depict them containing a wide range of marketable products, including pearl necklaces, handkerchiefs, ostrich feathers, purses and powder horns. It was the provost's duty to set up a marketplace where, with the help of the proviantmeister and the quartermaster, food and other goods were made available to the Landsknechts. The provost had to keep order, set fair prices (not too high, thereby causing unrest, yet not too low, for fear that the traders would stay away). In return for providing safe trading surroundings and protection for the traders, he received a 'cut' of the goods on offer; for example, the tongue of every animal sold, a measure of every vat of wine or beer traded or a percentage of money that changed hands. He also received percentages of the other 'services' (whores, gamblers, etc) on offer; even the prisoners, who were normally held in his tent, had to pay him for their board and lodging. Obviously then the position brought with it considerable enrichment but was also open to abuse. The wise provost therefore made sure that the common Landsknecht was well cared for and not subjected to unfair practice, while keeping a firm hand on all aspects of camp life. In his day-to-day work the provost was supported by the *hurenweibel* (whores' sergeant) who, as his name suggests, was responsible for keeping order amongst the train; the *stockmeister* (master of the stocks), who, with his helpers, the *steckenknechte* was responsible for guarding prisoners, and the *nachrichter*, also known as *scharfrichter* (executioner), known as the 'free man', who, apparently dressed in a plain red doublet and with a large red feather in his hat, would walk around the camp with his executioner's sword by his side and carry the hangman's noose in his hand as a symbol of his office. This jolly figure was no doubt avoided and would hardly have been a merry drinking partner!

On a more local level, the new recruits would already know the officers of their individual fähnlein: the captain, his representative and second-in-command, the lieutenant and the ensign. The captain, like the colonel, was entitled to a staff and bodyguards and would have cut a magnificent figure, clad in full 'knightly' armour and armed in the manner of the doppelsöldner with poleaxe and halbard or two-handed

Landsknechts at play. When off duty, Landsknechts and Reisläufer could be fairly difficult neighbours. At times such heavily armed revellers could turn a petty squabble into all-out war. Decent folk were appalled, and this satirical print shows drunken soldiers vomiting, playing dice with the devil and setting about each other with swords and daggers. (Eli Tanner/TMAG)

sword. Unlike the colonel, however, the captain would fight on foot, as would the rest of the leaders of the fähnlein. A figure that would have been viewed by the new recruit with considerable esteem was the ensign. He was usually chosen by the colonel and was second in importance only to the captain; each fähnlein had one. In later periods, when the use of firearms was more prevalent, ensigns tended to be 'cannon fodder' and were usually young boys who could easily be replaced. In this period, however, these men were chosen for their size and their courage and skill in battle, and their position carried enormous prestige and importance. Their role was to take care of the banner but, far more importantly, to form the nucleus of the fähnlein, the rallying point in battle, the centre of the camp and a focal point for the distribution of orders. He was usually accompanied by the *spiel*, the fifers and drummers, who would also march in the centre of the *gevierthaufen* (pike square). From the moment the banner was formally presented to the fähnlein's ensign during the muster, this flag and its carrier became the very symbol of the unit's 'manliness, courage and being'. The banner was never to fall into enemy hands; in battle the ensign would forfeit his life if he dropped it and ran; on the march or in quarters he would be liable to the worst mockery if he should lose it or allow it to be stolen.

So important was the banner that at the battle of Marignano in 1515, a dead Landsknecht ensign was found with both his arms chopped off and part of the banner pole clenched between his teeth. His banner had obviously just been captured by the Confederates, who 'had beaten and struck dead many of the enemy, in particular their Landsknechts. From them the Confederates had captured 12 Fähnlein, which were paraded in triumph through their ranks.' On the second day of the battle, the

Landsknechts exacted their revenge, and symbolically mistreated a captured Confederate banner on the battlefield: 'a green Fähnlein was eaten by the Landsknechts, chopped up in a salad'. Banners were such a powerful symbol that heroic deeds would be done to capture them, and, when captured, they were very valuable trophies. In 1527, after the storming of Bosco, 'the Confederates sent three captured Landsknecht Fähnlein home to their superiors, to avoid arguments over the sharing out.'

Unlike in later armies, however, the ensign was not required to lead from the front, except in extremis, when his intervention could well save the fähnlein from complete destruction. In a normal attack, the banners would be carried in the centre of the pike block; in the front rank they would have been a hindrance rather than a help, and in any case the ensign would have had great difficulty defending himself in the chaos of points and blades. Several sources mention the ensign giving his banner to his bodyguard once the order of battle had been made and then striding amongst the ranks, giving encouragement and comfort, before returning to his place. While the banner would usually fly in the presence of the enemy, illustrations show the ensign of a beaten unit furling the flag as a symbol of 'enough for today' and shouldering the pole for a quick retreat. In hopeless situations, tearing the banner to pieces was the only solution. In recognition of his importance, the ensign would be paid as much as six *sold* (24 guilders).

Every fähnlein had a *feldweibel* (sergeant major), who was the lowest of the officers selected by the colonel (other leaders were usually selected by the officers or voted into office by the soldiers). The feldweibel was an 'elderly, honest, experienced man', who had already served as a *rottmeister*, *gemeinweibel* or *führer*. He was the drill master, with the responsibility of setting up the order of battle, of ensuring that the soldiers knew their place in line, and of manoeuvring the *gevierthaufen*. Unfortunately there are few records of formal drill from this period, and most historians seem to think that manoeuvring was an informal, slapdash affair. However, with a pike square made up of thousands of men, it would have been impossible to move the force in a disciplined way without considerable training and standardised commands. There are several clues as to the existence of drill. Firstly, the Landsknecht mode of close-combat fighting was modelled on the armies of the Helvetic Confederation. It is known that troops from the various cantons that made up the Confederation would muster on public holidays 'and train in the use of the pike in the manner of their forefathers'. Pictures from the *Schilling Chronicles* show perfectly aligned ranks and files of men marching in step, with the same shoulder forward. Also, the constant fighting and feuding in this part of Europe would have meant

Bernese banner bearer, Master C.S. c.1500. This proud ensign from the City of Bern wears a typical Reisläufer turban and panoply of ostrich plumes. His clothes are neatly and decoratively slashed, the slashes are clearly not random cuts made to make tight-fitting garments an easier fit. His hugely exaggerated *baselard* (hilted sword) hangs between his legs, a silent advertisement of his virility. The original print is uncoloured but he probably wore the black and red colours of Bern. The Bernese flag was, and still is, red with a diagonal deep yellow bar bearing a black bear. (Eli Tanner)

Banner Bearers, by Urs Graf, c.1516. It is not always easy to read the visual messages included in the drawings and caricatures of this period. Urs Graf in particular included many symbolic features, some no longer understood by us. On the left, a regimental banner bearer struts along with his soldier servant following with tonight's looted dinner. The banner bearer on the right carries a banner, which is perhaps the red and white flag of the Helvetic Confederation, but almost hidden in the dark ground colour of the flag are fleurs-de-lys, dice and Confederate crosses. He wears an extra hat slung behind his back, and his shoes are not a matching pair. Is Urs Graf trying to ridicule the ragged affectations of the campaigning soldier or the simple Confederate mercenary with a foot in both French and Imperial camps? (private collection)

that any young man worth his salt would have trained in the use of the pike and the halbard from the moment he could walk, so the methodology of this warfare would have been perfected and passed from generation to generation. Secondly, since a pikeman is practically useless on his own, and a stationary mass of pikes of value only in defence, the essence of this type of warfare was to present a mass of levelled pike tips in the form of an *igel* (hedgehog) and to be able to manoeuvre this 'hedgehog' effectively around the battlefield.

The author knows from personal experience that even untrained troops will quickly learn to march in step when a competent drummer is present and that even large units can be easily manoeuvred with a very basic set of commands. The drummers would have played the drums, with easily recognisable sets of rhythms being used to transmit orders, pass messages and even send insults to the opposing armies! (To understand this, the reader should visit the Basel Fastnacht and listen to the complex drumming of passages – very different from the African and South American rhythmic repetition of a single beat that the modern ear is used to.) Perhaps drill was so commonplace and simple

Reisläufer musicians, by Urs Graf, 1523. It is of interest to note the fife case, French fleur-de-lys badge and katzbalger of the figure on the right. Urs Graf has added a laughing animal to the sleeve of the figure centre left. Music has always been vitally important to the military. Published in 1589, *Orchesography*, written by Thoinot Arbeau, is the most detailed record of 15th- and 16th-century dances to have survived. Fortunately for students of military music, Arbeau and his contemporaries saw dance as suitable exercise for young men and soldiers and described the instruments used for marching: 'long trumpets, trumpets, bugles, clarinets, horns, cornets, flutes, fifes, pipes, drums, the "Persian" drum, used on horse by the Germans (kettle-drum)', and the deep military drum used by the French, which made 'a great noise'. Many 15th-century illustrations show the Swiss and Germans marching on campaign and into battle to fife, drum and bagpipe, but Arbeau is the first source to describe the soldiers being made to march to certain rhythms, in step and starting with the same (left) foot. This was almost certainly already a long-established tradition. It is impossible to imagine an army of pikemen marching in close formation without keeping step, especially when music is being played. Arbeau also stated that the drummer played the rhythm while the fifer improvised. (Öffentliche Kunstsammlung, Basel)

that the chroniclers did not bother to record it, but the fact that we have no drill books from this period does not mean that they did not exist. Moreover, the grizzled veteran, the feldweibel, would certainly have understood how to manoeuvre the gevierthaufen (a square formation that consisted of several thousand pikemen, with halbardiers, drummers, fifers and banners in the centre) without the lot turning into a disorganised rabble. Since the gevierthaufen was made up of ranks (*glieder*) and files (*rotten*), the importance of the doppelsöldner, who made up approximately one-quarter of every fähnlein, in this manoeuvring cannot be stressed enough. These experienced men always made up the front *glied*, effectively taking up the front position of every file. When carrying out the more complex manoeuvres, such as wheeling or re-aligning the front of the formation, the soldiers following in the files had only to follow the lead of elite doppelsöldner in the front rank. Further doppelsöldner in the rear ranks, interspersed in the formation, would help to keep the formation together and ensure that

21

dotted more like assvers than sergt
rank and
file

the less experienced troops would know where to go (no doubt with much 'shouting and blows').

To help maintain the structure of the gevierthaufen, each fähnlein's feldweibel was supported by (usually) two *gemeinweibel* (common sergeants), who would take up their place at either end of the front glied. These doppelsöldner, armed usually with a spear or halbard rather than a pike in view of their workload, and with a sash or a particularly rich set of feathers as a distinguishing mark, would ensure that the order of the formation was kept when marching in the order of battle. Their role in camp was to represent the interests of the rank and file in dealings with the colonel and the provost, and help with the distribution of supplies to the rottmeister, the doppelsöldner chosen to lead each of the files. In a typical fähnlein square of, say, 400 men (20 ranks and 20 files), each rottmeister would have responsibility for approximately 20 men. These, and other junior officers such as the führer (apparently a type of defence lawyer or *fürsprech* [literally 'for-speak'] who would represent the rank and file at the schultheiss court) and the *fourier* (who defended the interests of the rank and file in the camp or quarters) were chosen for a period of one month by the common soldiers in an open vote.

CAMP LIFE

Law and Discipline

Life in camp was subject to a rigid set of laws, with a proper legal system in place to enforce them and administer punishment. The usual image of Landsknecht life is one of lawlessness and impromptu justice, but the opposite was in fact the case. Unique in German military history were the special privileges accorded to the Landsknecht class. These privileges, given by Maximilian as part of his new military order, meant that the Landsknechts were not subject to civil law, and could set and enforce their own legal system as a co-operative. Although the main principles of civil law were obviously applied, with a court system to rule over right and wrong and decide on punishment, and with the powerful figure of the colonel, armed with the power of veto, as the ultimate judicial power, the system of justice lay ultimately in the hands of the common Landsknecht, and only the most determined officer would have risked going against the wishes of the soldiers.

Here in fact it immediately becomes apparent that the most powerful weapon available to the

Gemeinwebel, woodcut, c.1530. This may represent a common Landsknecht voted into the position of sergeant by his fellow troops for a period of one month. Hence spear and authoritative pose, but no armour. (J.R.)

Mortal Combat, by Paul Dolstein, c.1500. Dolstein has drawn what appears to be a dismounted Swedish knight fighting at close quarters with a very confident Landsknecht. (Thür. Hauptstaatsarchiv, Weimar)

colonel was the power to dispense pay; as mentioned previously, when funds were available discipline was easy to enforce. When pay dried up, as was so often the case, the legal system could swiftly break down. The civil court system depended on a judge (schultheiss), supported by lay judges (schöffen), who would hear the merits of a case and decide the outcome of the trial. The military schultheiss court differed in the larger number of people directly involved in the decision-making process and also in the involvement of the common soldiers.

The schultheiss court followed a strict ceremonial course. The event took place in public and in the open air, usually at the central mustering area (*alarmplatz*) of the camp. Those of the Landsknecht community who wanted to be present would arrive only lightly armed and stand in a large circle around the court bench. They were obliged under strict penalty to observe the peace and solemnity of the court and appear as observers only. On the main bench, the schultheiss sat with his attendant scribe; on either side, on benches set up in the form of a square or rectangle, were seated the court members responsible for the verdict. Sources generally state that there were 24 of them, consisting of up to 12 schöffen (in this case specially chosen doppelsöldner who represented each of the fähnlein), captains, ensigns, sergeants and führers (the direct representatives of the common soldiers). The colonel or his representative could also take part if he wanted to. In every case it was the provost who acted as the prosecutor, and both he and the defendant could be represented by an advocate. Both parties were also entitled to *zween räth* (two counsellors). This modern-sounding system was all the more remarkable for the fact that defendants in earlier feudal courts had usually been judged by their 'betters'. The judgement (usually) by their peers drew a good deal of attention in contemporary literature.

The process had to be completed in three consecutive days and there was no appeal against the verdict. If the defendant was found guilty, punishment was meted out immediately, and if he or she had been sentenced to death, the execution was usually carried out there and then by the sword or the noose of the nachrichter.

A particular form of self-justice peculiar to Landsknecht armies was the 'pike court'. This type of court was essentially different from the schultheiss court in that it was not automatically a privilege of the regiment. During the initial mustering of the regiment, the pike court had to be recognised by the warlord and then accepted by the majority of the soldiers in an open vote. This type of court must have been considered a useful, ritual act of 'letting off steam, otherwise it would never have been accepted by the troops. It was only used when the defendant had openly and obviously damaged the order in the regiment or brought disgrace upon the flag, and there was no question as to his guilt. In such a case, presumably to avoid the long-winded process of examining the evidence, the provost could ask the colonel for permission to proceed. Only then could he assemble the community, who would then vote on whether the court should continue. Since the defendant appeared directly in front of the assembled regiment, and all decisions would be taken directly by the troops, there was no need for a bench or judges. Since the verdict could only be death or acquittal, the entire process, including voting and execution, had to be carried out in one day. Like the schultheiss court, a verdict was reached after evidence and counter-evidence had been presented by the advocates of the provost and the defendant. When the evidence had been heard, the provost would reiterate his call for the death penalty, while the defendant would beg for leniency. Three separate groups of Landsknechts would now decide on a verdict independently of each other and present the result. The assembled troops thus had three independent recommendations to help them make their final decision, which was made by majority vote. If a guilty verdict was returned, the soldiers would move to the place of execution, where they formed up in two lines of three ranks each, in an east–west direction, with the ensigns closing the gap at the end, standing with their backs to the sun. The delinquent would walk three times between the lines, begging for forgiveness and also giving it, before taking up his position at the end, next to the provost. The provost would strike him three times on the

Stradioti, based on the work of Urs Graf, c.1515. These mercenary light cavalry came from what is now Yugoslavia, Albania and Greece, and were employed mostly by the Venetian Republic. Their 'top hats', long hanging sleeves, curved swords, lances and composite Turkish bows were caricatured by the artists who saw them. They were fierce, outlandishly dressed and over-fond of plunder. (Öffentliche Kunstsammlung, Basel/TMAG)

right shoulder and ask him to run swiftly between the lines, where his 'honest' comrades, to the sound of drums and fifes, would finish his life with the points of their pikes. Any comrade who left a gap for the delinquent to escape 'would step into his shoes'.

THE TRAIN

When a Landsknecht army entered the field, it was followed by an enormous train of wagons, supplies and hangers-on. In a period when the organisational facilities of the state could just about supply enough finance to pay the *sold* and furnish the artillery and ancillary heavy siege equipment, the components of the train were based on the personal requirements of the individual soldiers, despite numerous attempts to regulate what followed the army. Later armies would have an organised system of supply columns as part of the army structure, but before the invention of refrigeration, no supply system could provide food in sufficient quantities and keep the perishable items long enough to satisfy the needs of the men, so even these armies were often forced to rely on what the land could provide. In the armies of the Landsknecht period, the train fulfilled that vital role of supplying food and comfort to the soldier with a fair degree of success, and was therefore tolerated. Its success was driven by the principle of supply and demand; when food ran low, prices went up and traders had more incentive to supply. Only when money ran out did disaster strike.

The *Sudler and the Sudlerin*, by Daniel Hopfer. The sudler was basically a contract cook, seen here with his partner, carrying the spoons and ladles of their trade. The word 'sudler' is derived from 'sud', meaning stock. The sudler would set up his cauldrons in the middle of the camp and boil 'sheep, goats, beef, pork, geese, sausages and sauerkraut', to sell to hungry soldiers. Note the lady's purse, and shoes with a long tongue, perhaps designed to protect the feet from splashes of boiling water. (N.M.)

Generally it can be assumed that there was a wagon for every ten soldiers in the army, to carry personal belongings, booty and supplies. The wealthier the Landsknecht, the more personal comforts would have been taken, with the wealthiest doppelsöldner being followed by wagons carrying tents, furniture, bedding, wall hangings and supplies for themselves, their wives, their personal servants and their families. Since each Landsknecht was to all intents and purposes a self-supporting entity (the army provided him with nothing except money), every soldier needed some personal support, someone to cook for him, set up the camp, mend and wash his clothing and nurse him when wounded or sick. Women and boys carried out this supporting role. In a set of the articles of war from 1530, it was proposed that two or three women should be engaged to be 'everyman's wife' and step in where needed. They were employed directly by the colonel, stood under his protection and were paid a fraction of the *sold*. They could improve their income with 'services of love' (per day, two *kreuzer*). Naturally there were also a large number of unofficial 'wives', and despite constant attempts to restrict the numbers of whores in the camp, the decision on whether to allow them was usually left to the colonel. Even children followed the army, and this great mass of humanity, of whores, traders, tinkers, cooks, sutlers, drivers and associated dross, could often fetter the movement of the army and pose its own threat to its discipline.

A typical camp kitchen, from a woodcut by Erhard Schön, c.1535. Contemporary illustrations like these deserve careful examination. They are full of details, from the soldiers playing dice on a drum in the background, to the sudlerin ladling out her soup. Note the tents, including a smoking kitchen tent and the rough shelters for supplies. Most illustrations of 15- and 16th-century camp kitchens show cauldrons slung from a branch across two Y-shaped supports. (private collection/TMAG)

The maintenance of law and order in the train was absolutely vital and the responsibility for it lay in the hands of the *hurenweibel* (whores' sergeant), whose name does nothing to convey the huge responsibility of his task. Not only was he in charge of the everyday organisation and policing of the train, but also had the tactical responsibility of manoeuvring the train when in the presence of the enemy, keeping it out of harm's way and avoiding being a hindrance to the fighting units. This highly experienced battle-scarred veteran fulfilled such a vital role that he was paid around the same as a captain (about 40 guilders per month). Supporting him were the *rumormeisters,* who would keep discipline by beating obstreperous women and boys with their *vergleicher* (argument settlers), which were 'sticks the length of an arm'. For the lower orders, the 'worst whores were the best wives', and life in the army must have been hard for most of the women, particularly as they were completely dependent on the men for their income. No doubt many of the lesser noblemen's wives were left with a hard choice when faced with the death of a husband, for the route home was long and dangerous. Army life had its compensations though, for the women had the opportunity to escape from otherwise quite drab lives and experience foreign climes. Naturally there was plenty of adventure to be had, and for the wealthier women at least, the fact that they were not subject to the sumptuary laws meant that they could dress as they pleased. The women and the boys carried out other vital jobs that were considered 'beneath' the Landsknechts, such as 'cleaning and sweeping the shitting places and digging entrenchments and fieldworks. In later times, the soldiers would come to realise that 'digging saves blood', but in this period it was the womenfolk who were the experts with the gabions and the *chevaux de frize.*

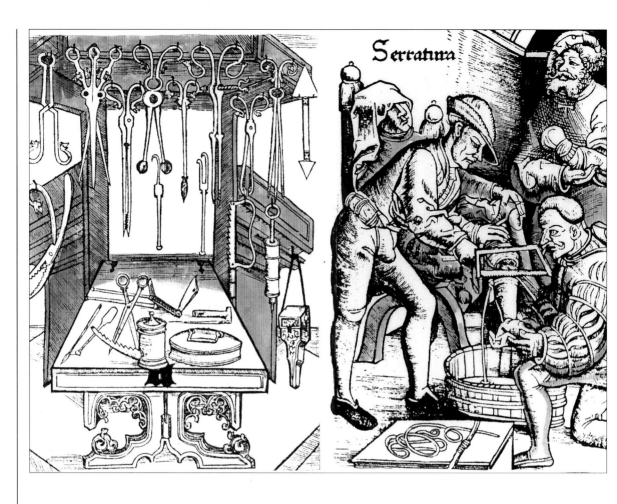

Sertatura

SICKNESS

The greatest cause of death in any mercenary army was not enemy action but sickness, and in any campaign quite large numbers of troops could be lost before ever seeing action. Early in 1524, 5,000 Confederate Reisläufer marched to reinforce Francis I's army camped near Milan and under threat from the Imperial forces. They arrived just in time to share in a complete disaster. Cut off from sources of supply by roadblocks, the army started to disintegrate. The Reisläufer marched home, but on the way 'a hard awful sickness overtook the Confederates on the road, so that of 12,000 men, only a third survived, returning in such a wretched state, that the roads into Fribourg and Bern were choked with straw-filled ladder wagons, filled with sick, dying and dead all piled together. It was such a piteous sight, that everybody said that it would be a warning, not to travel in unlucky countries. In June 1527 the ragged, demoralised Imperial Spanish/German army that had just sacked Rome was practically wiped out by the plague. Georg von Frundsburg, returning to Mindelheim after suffering a stroke in the camp near Bologna, heard that his son Melchior was among the dead. In the spring of 1528, a Reisläufer contingent of 4,000 Bernese was practically wiped out by the plague, along with most of the French army on the march to Naples.

Surgeons and their instruments. At this time, medical treatment in some areas was surprisingly sophisticated; in others, it could be extremely brutal. In 1514 Antonio Ferri, physician to the Pope, published a work recommending that gunshot wounds should be treated with boiling oil and a fast amputation carried out with a hatchet, followed by the application of a red-hot iron to the stump. At the other extreme, the incredible suffering of the wounded revolted a French military surgeon, Ambroise Paré, who gained much experience with the army of Francis I in Italy. He tried many alternative treatments, which included careful amputation using a knife and saw, tying off of the arteries, and a great deal more care and rest for the wounded than was usual. (JR/TMAG)

RELIGION

Naturally, every fähnlein would have a chaplain to look after its spiritual well-being. Their role was to assemble the troops in the morning in front of the captain's tent at least several days a week and preach the gospel. Before battle, the chaplains would lead the prayers and afterwards dispense comfort to the wounded and the last rites to the dying. However, sources from the period state that 'Christian, clever, honourable men would seldom be found among the ranks of the chaplains', and their relatively low pay of only 8 guilders would seem to bear this out. Their low standing was no doubt due to the fact that, in a time of religious revolution (the Reformation) and religious wars, religious beliefs had remarkably little effect on the allegiances of the Landsknechts. During the Schmalkal Wars, Protestant princes of lower Germany were unsuccessful in recruiting large numbers of mercenaries despite strong Protestant sympathies among the Landsknechts. This was mainly due to the fact that the Landsknechts 'were neither the enemy of the Emperor, nor did they want to take up arms for Warlords against whom they had previously fought'. Emperor Maximilian himself was most careful to avoid religious confrontations, and,

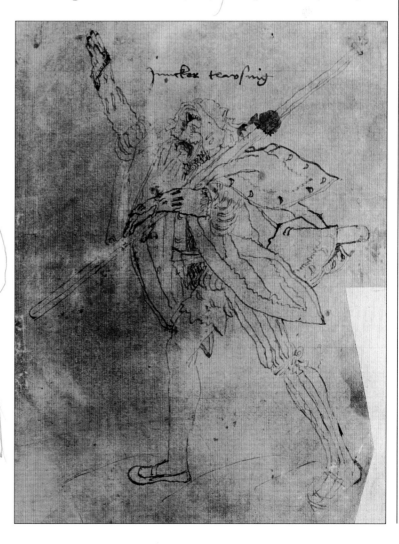

Doppelsöldner on the March, by Paul Dolstein, c.1500. Junker Treusing (or Trausing) struts along, ragged but proud. Wrapped in a short gown, he has pulled his cap around his ears against the cold. (Thür. Hauptstaatsarchiv, Weimar)

despite being a Catholic, not only allowed Protestant chaplains in his armies, but also paid them. The indifference to religion can also be explained by the fact that during this period the Catholic Emperor and kings of the Habsburg Empire were fighting the Catholic kings of France for dominance of Europe. Both sides recruited mercenaries from Protestant areas. Although Charles V had outlawed Martin Luther at the Imperial Diet of Worms in 1521, his own troops carried out the atrocity of the sacking of Rome two years after the triumph of Pavia. Not only was the Pope considered the enemy of the Landsknechts because he had joined the anti-Imperial coalition, but the Emperor, unable to pay his Spanish/German mercenaries, sent them against the Holy Father on purpose, hoping they would find the missing pay in large quantities. Needless to say, the tired, demoralised, ragged troops, in spite of their religious beliefs, had no trouble in helping themselves to the Pope's rich plunder.

COSTUME

The Origin of Slashing

The most obvious outward sign of a mercenary, both Landsknecht and Helvetic Reisläufer, was his mode of dress. The increasingly slashed fashion was always considered slightly shocking to contemporary sensibilities, and the Landsknecht fashion of uncovering the upper legs and the prominent codpiece were all intended to shock and remind the observer of the independence of the mercenary. Anshelm records in 1503 that as a result of the Helvetic Reisläufer influence, the civilian fashions had changed over the previous ten years and

now, all clothing has changed for man and woman. They come with shaggy hats or storm-baretts, with skirts and long coats, with many folds and widely-cut, wide sleeves, doublets with slashes, with woolen, wide decorated collars and wide breast panel, cut-outs at the armpit, with silver buttons around and in front; silk doublets [here he notes with some disapproval that even the peasants had started to wear silk]; high, one-piece hose seat, stuffed, large codpiece, one piece legs, divided lengthways in strips of different colour and held with ribbons; white, widely-cut shirts; they come now, dressed only in doublet and hose, which is a great scandal; wide cut-out shoes, with or without rings, with long decorated 'Schweizerdegen' or curved falchions, with large bi-spike or bi-knife, with daggers and closed pouches, with purses around the neck, in the doublet or in the codpiece, with large plumes of ostrich feathers and short hair, often close shaved.

The origin of the slashed fashion is difficult to trace, and various ideas have been put forward for its evolution. It has often been suggested that the Landsknechts copied their fantastic mode of dress from the Helvetic Confederates, and there is some evidence for this, at least where the use of colourful material is concerned. Slashing, however, only really started to appear in contemporary illustrations about ten years after it should have done if Landsknechts had truly copied the Confederates at the zenith of their military power. The Confederates captured enormous quantities of fabulously rich cloth from the Burgundians at the battles of Grandson and Murten, and much of it was distributed among the common soldiers. The use of this cloth in the manufacture of wonderfully lavish and colourful costume must have certainly been a way of demonstrating the fact that a soldier had taken part in those battles and would have been an enormous source of pride. This military fashion would then have been widely copied by those civilians who could afford it.

Off-duty Reisläufer. A very fine reconstruction of a costume c.1515 made by Marina Harrington for Nick Michael of the Company of St George. Note the voluminous sleeves. This Reisläufer has slipped his doublet off his shoulders but, still retained at the waist by laces, it hangs around his hips, a style common in the 15th and 16th centuries and a quick and convenient way to cool down in hot weather. (John Howe)

Landsknecht officer, woodcut by Niklas Meldemann and David de Negker. He wears the three-quarter armour typical of a doppelsöldner and his spear and sash probably point this fellow out as a feldwebel (sergeant major). His cropped hair, long beard and rakishly tilted flat cap were fashionable in this period. Note his dagger hanging on chains from his waist belt but apparently tied down to his thigh like a Western gun fighter. The hilt of his katzbalger sword has, unusually, a guard. (private collection)

After 1477, Confederates and Landsknechts fought for the same warlords until the events of the end of the century turned them into implacable enemies, and certainly there was ample scope for the cross-fertilisation of clothing fashions. Illustrations before 1505 show an increasing complexity in the use of colour. Yellow, red, light and medium blue, medium green, pink, grey, white and black were all popular. Whereas hose of 1477 might have been *mi-partie* (each leg a different colour), by 1505 each leg of the hose would have been made of ever-narrower strips of alternating colour, although it was rare that more than two or three complementary colours were used in a particular costume.

However, true slashing really only started to appear at the beginning of the Italian Wars, and it was no doubt copied from the civilian fashions of the city noblemen of northern Italy (contemporary Italian illustrations show this fashion from about 1480 onwards, while it first appears in German and Helvetic illustrations after 1500). There is no evidence to suggest that it was used to make the clothing easier to move in (after all, clothing and especially hose had been skin-tight and therefore pretty flexible for almost a century) or to enable smaller captured costume to fit larger men. Nor was it meant to be a count of how many times the soldier had suffered a near miss! The large slashed sleeves could in fact get tangled in the weaponry, particularly with the large double-handed swords seen in many illustrations and must have disintegrated fairly swiftly in the continuous skirmishing of an average campaign. The illustrator Urs Graf shows marvellous 'before and after' pictures of campaigning mercenaries, with the returning soldier dressed in tatters. To stop the clothing disappearing of its own accord, slashing depends on the use of cloth that does not fray, and good-quality felted wool cloth is ideal for this. It is therefore fair to assume that this was the outer material of choice, while the linings that became ever more voluminous could be coloured linen, silk or damask.

No matter what the origins, the flamboyant dress was important for the esprit de corps. Emperor Maximilian, when challenged by one of his noblemen as to why a soldier of lowly origins was allowed to wear such rich clothing when civilian dress was regulated by sumptuary laws, is quoted as saying, 'leave them be; with their wretched and miserable existence you should not begrudge them a little fun'. In fact, after the defeat of the peasants in the Peasant Wars, the Imperial Diet of Worms in 1530 tried to stop the emancipation of the lower orders by laying down strict codes of dress for the various classes. Even the knights, noblemen and princes were limited in the 'amount of gold and silver they could attach to their velvet and silk clothing' and in the value of the gold chains around their necks (a count, for example, was limited to chain with a value of 500 guilders and was not allowed to wear clothing with a sable lining). The Landsknecht, however, being 'a man of war in service or with a captain on the march, and this being proven by a passport or certificate', was able to 'dress and wear his clothes in any way he sees fit'.

The basic structure of clothing had remained unchanged for most of the 15th century. When dressing for the day, the average male would start with a pair of braes (loose linen underpants) and a linen shirt. The most common style of shirt was a voluminous affair gathered into a band at the neck, sometimes secured with a simple band or button but more often with a drawstring. So large were the shirts that at the battle of Pavia, Georg von Frundsberg was able to get his troops to wear their shirts over the rest of their clothing as a recognition sign, and contemporary illustrations show the shirt reaching almost to the knees. As the 16th century progressed, more of the shirt became visible and the collars became increasingly ornate, ultimately turning into the ruffs of the 17th century. In warm weather the shirt was sometimes worn open to the point of the shoulder. Over the braes came a pair of tight hose, made of a very flexible woollen material (possibly knitted) and increasingly decorated as the century progressed. Up to about 1550, the hose legs included the feet. Once the hose was slashed (usually above the knee), a ribbon was tied just below the knee, which stopped the hose sagging and allowed the slashing to open up, displaying the lining. During the early campaigns in the Netherlands and Denmark, as well as the Italian campaigns, it became very fashionable to cut the hose off completely just above the knee, leaving the lining dangling like a strange apron. The lower part of the hose was then held up with ribbons, pointed back on to the upper part again, or dispensed with altogether. Just after the siege of Montfort in 1491, when Duke Albrecht von Sachsen was fighting in the Netherlands and was outnumbered by the enemy, Wilwort von Schaumburg and other officers 'climbed off their horses and in order to encourage their men, kept their breast and back plates and their collars on, cut their hose off and stood with the troops in the front rank'. Similar things were recounted of a Captain Neidhart Fuchs, who later fought with Duke Albrecht in Friesland. Instructions by Hans Weiditz to the painter of the 'Fürstenburg Shield' (Historical Museum Bern) state: 'Item Fürstenberg with two figures, one carrying halbard; with slashed clothing, cut-off hose and large feather plume'. Why the hose was cut in this way is not known, but it was very common among the Landsknechts. Speculation that it was to improve ease of movement of the left leg (the leg that is bent most when kneeling with a pike) is probably unfounded, as the right leg is also often seen 'freed'. In the early years of the 16th century, the Confederates are also often shown with cut-off hose, but the usage gradually disappears, which would be unusual if hose was too restrictive. The fashion lasted longer with the Landsknechts, finally dying out as the *pluderhosen* took over.

The Landsknechts were also increasingly seen in breeches, a type of secondary hose worn over the normal hose and which allowed further opportunities for decoration, while dispensing with the technical

Costume

A

Siege of Tunis, 1535

D

Reisläufer on the March, Marignano Campaign, 1515

E

Frundsberg Recruiting Landsknechts for
the Pavia Campaign of 1525

F

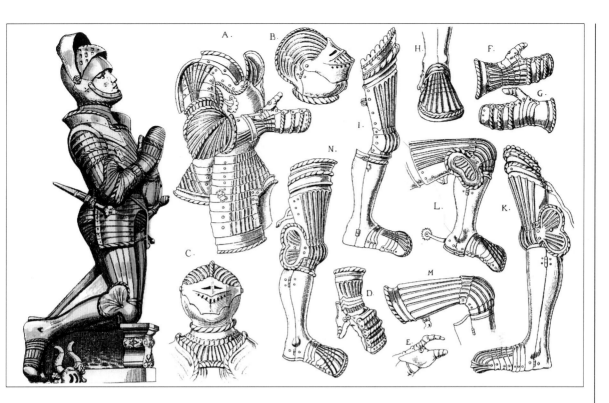

The effigy of George von Liebenstein, a German knight who died in 1533, and a contemporary drawing of the parts of a similar armour. A. back and breast plates with arm and gauntlet; B. armet, a helmet which completely enclosed the head; C. front view of the armet, sitting and swiveling on the plate collar to which were attached the arms; D.– G. four views of the gauntlets; H. articulated plates that follow the shape of the fashionable shoe; I. the inside view of the left leg; K. the outside view of the left leg, L. outside view of the right leg. Full armour like this might have been worn by senior officers such as feldobristen, obristen and locotenents when mounted. (private collection)

difficulty of keeping a separate lower hose secured in some way (most boy scouts will remember the difficulty of keeping their socks up). Paul Dolnstein shows an early Landsknecht wearing breeches over hose in the 1490s, Mätthaus Konrad Schwarz describes wearing them in 1523, and they are also mentioned in the accounts of the Saxon court tailor as 'breeches over fighting hose'. After 1550, these breeches gradually evolved into the *pluderhosen*, while the lower part of the hose was often replaced with silk stockings. These were very expensive (they had to be imported from the Orient) and remained, at least to start with, the exclusive domain of the nobleman or the soldier who had done well in plunder. As the prices came down at the end of the century, the stocking became the rule rather than the exception. Even the codpiece became more and more ornate, and increasingly prominent. By the middle of the century it had become so large that it was often used to store the purse and other personal items. In 1555 Bishop Musculus of Frankfurt notes that 'our young friends stuff their codpieces with hell-fire and rags and make them so big that the devil can sit in them and look out on all sides, purely as an annoyance and bad example, yes even for the temptation and seduction of poor, witless and innocent young girls.'

Over the shirt came a doublet, a garment that could be very tight-fitting indeed around the torso (almost a foundation garment) as long as there was plenty of material around the top of the arm and under the arm-pit. Doublet and hose were then fastened together with points (a type of lace with metal tips resembling modern shoelaces), mainly to keep the hose up but also to keep the doublet taut. Since it was rare for the common soldier to wear a gown or coat (these would presumably travel on the wagon and be used in camp), the doublet would be lined with a certain amount of padding to keep out the cold and provide some protection.

The pointed shoes of the late 15th century had given way to the wide shoes resembling *kuhmäule* (cow mouths) or *bärentatzen* (bear's paws), which became ever more minimalistic as the 16th century progressed. Indeed, some illustrations show shoes with so little overlap over the front of the toes and at the heel that they could only have been sewn to the hose. On his head the Landsknecht would wear one of the myriad designs of *barett* (a type of large beret), often over a coif or metal skullcap and almost invariably decorated with feathers.

Subtle costume variation as a mark of regional identity

As mentioned at the beginning of this book, the Landsknecht armies had been raised in the image of the Helvetic Confederates and much of the costume style was taken from them. There were, however, many subtle differences that set the two apart. Nowadays it is difficult when looking at contemporary illustrations to spot these differences immediately, but in a period of intense rivalry spanning nearly a century, these differences were immediately apparent to the people of the day. Illustrators of the period constantly pointed out these differences, and, indeed, in setting themselves apart in dress and manner, each group effectively drew the lines that we now know as national boundaries. A traveller on his way from London to Bern would have noted many different clothing styles and would no doubt have been recognised, if not as an Englishman, then at least as a foreigner. French fashion, based on the stricter, more conservative court fashions, would have been more sober, whilst German fashions, based on the Landsknecht lead, were very flamboyant. Italian fashions were a mixture of

Young Confederate nobleman and wife, pen drawing by Niklaus Manuel Deutsch, c.1515. This ultra-fashionable young civilian couple's clothes are almost indistinguishable from those worn by their more military-minded contemporaries. (Öffentliche Kunstsammlung, Basel)

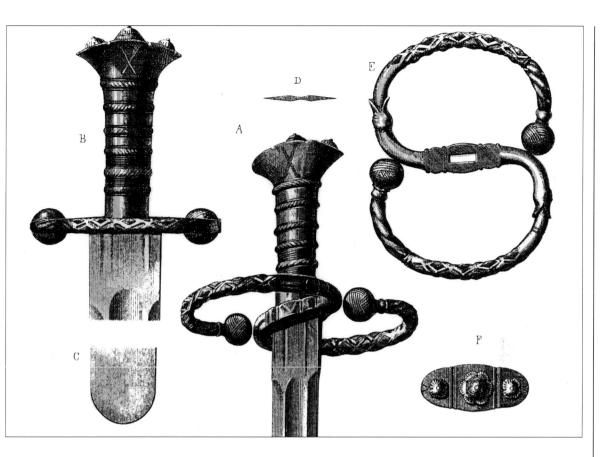

Landsknecht katzbalger. This illustration shows the component parts of the Landsknecht's favourite weapon, the katzbalger. 'Katz' means cat, while 'balgen' means to scrap, so a rough translation would be 'weapon for a fight with tooth and claw'. A. and B., the hilt marked with the Burgundian St Andrew's cross, a practical design that did not slip easily from the hand; C. the tip of the blade, frequently rounded and sharp; D. section through the blade; E. characteristic S-shaped quillons; F. top of pommel. (private collection)

the two, whilst Confederate clothing, although providing the lead for the outrageous Landsknecht style, never went as far, and was held back no doubt by the strong French influence.

All areas, however, shared the lively interest in clothing of the Renaissance. Among hundreds of sources that bear this out, the 'little clothing book' of Matthäus and Veit Konrad Schwarz is of particular interest. The father and son team, who were both citizens of Augsburg and both worked one after the other as accountants for the Fugger family (and were therefore certainly not short of money), thought their clothing so important that they prepared a book showing themselves in various outfits. The introduction by Veit Konrad Schwarz shows how strong the contemporary fascination with the unusual was. 'We Germans have always been like monkeys with our clothing – whatever we see we have to copy, no matter what the national style. No style of clothing is too adventurous for me, because the more unusual the cut of hose, doublet and shoes, the more likely I am to wear it.' The illustrations and descriptions contained in the book more than bear this out.

The best way to examine the everyday apparel of the Landsknecht is through the artwork of the time. The reader should remember that we are looking at perhaps the birth of advertising, for the Landsknechts were in fact competing with the Confederate Reisläufer (Confederate mercenary) for a portion of an enormous pot of money. The Holy Roman Empire and France were competing for territory and in so doing, were competing for the services of the best troops available. Stradiots (fierce Venetian horsemen from the Balkans), Spanish

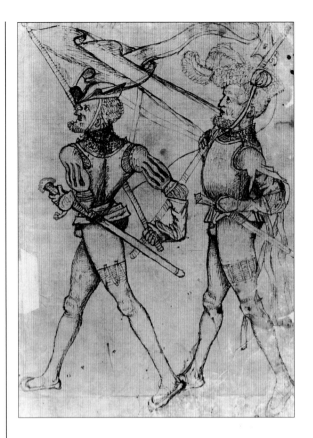

arquebus and sword-and-buckler troops and French troops all competed for lucrative contracts, but the main players, the most sought-after and reliable troops, were without doubt the Confederate Reisläufer and, to an increasing degree, the Landsknechts.

Illustrations were printed in large numbers for the first time (the printing press had only just been invented), and pictures showing the heroic deeds of the two rivals were displayed in public places. Many government officials and noblemen received 'pensions' from the two sides, in order to secure positive responses, and of course the obrists would stand to gain from a successful recruitment. It was therefore in their best interests to show their side in the best possible light. When making a political or propaganda point, the best way to make a figure instantly recognisable to the observer was to stress and perhaps exaggerate the typical characteristic look of each of the competing groups. Niklaus Manuel, in his illustration of 1529, does exactly this (see p.47). On the one hand, we have the Landsknecht, instantly recognisable by virtue of his close-shaved head, his moustache and 'goatee' beard and his short, wide-bladed katzbalger sword. The leather jerkin over the doublet, the cut-off hose (both legs bare) with the lining dangling below, together with the remainder of the hose legs held up by enormous ribbons contrive to make a stereotype that was immediately recognisable. On the other hand we have the Reisläufer, evidently a younger man, with a magnificent head of hair and side-burns, his barett decorated with a huge mass of ostrich feathers (the Reisläufer love of ostrich feathers and their air of superiority led the Landsknechts to call them federhansen [feather johnnies], among other things), the

Landsknechts, by Paul Dolstein, c.1500. Carrying what are perhaps the banners of Dolstein's fähnlein, two ensigns strut out escorted by halbardiers. There are many details of costume carefully depicted that are worth careful study and comparison with later drawings. Of particular interest are the 'shorts' of the first two figures, the lower hose laced to the upper and the curious loops of lace on three of their hats (a field sign perhaps?). Note the upper and lower sleeves held in place with laces reminiscent of late 15th-century Italian fashion. (Thür. Hauptstaatsarchiv, Weimar)

Landsknechts on the march, by Hans Sebald Beham, c.1540. Beham shows a good selection of well-armed foot soldiers. Of particular interest are the hats, worn at a rakish tilt, and the way in which the pikes and the halbards are carried. It is also of interest to note that the outer men always carry their weapons facing outward, and that the outer men of the rank of pikemen wear the full foot armour of the doppelsöldner. (private collection)

wide neck of the doublet and the slashing on the chest revealing a high-quality shirt, while the intact hose, slashed again to show the lining, and the more restrained ribbons contrast with the 'wilder' look of the Landsknecht. The elegant hand-and-a-half sword and the Confederate cross, neatly cut into the left sleeve, leave no doubt as to the provenance of the figure.

The ultimate symbol of the Confederacy, the *schweizerdolch* (Swiss dagger) is no doubt worn on the back of the belt, invisible in this case to the observer, but is drawn as part of Niklaus Manuel's signature at the bottom, proving the artist's allegiance beyond a doubt. Manuel was of course a Confederate with strong French sympathies and this explains the subtle difference between the noble, upright stance of the Reisläufer and the somewhat more pinched and disreputable appearance of the Landsknecht.

The hundreds of illustrations available show some other obvious differences between the two sides. Firstly the wearing of crosses clearly defines the allegiance of the wearer. The 'X' so often slit into the clothing of the Landsknecht is the cross of St Andrew, based on the Burgundian coat of arms inherited by Maximilian I and applied as livery to 'his' Landsknechts. The vertical cross worn on Reisläufer clothing is of course the easily recognisable Swiss cross in the modern flag and symbol of the old Confederacy. Other symbolic items never worn by Reisläufer are the katzbalger, the broad short sword with the guard in the form of an eight, and the peacock feather, symbol of the Habsburgs. On the Reisläufer

Landsknechts on the march, woodcuts by Necker, 1520, 1530. These convincing figures show Landsknecht costume modified for cold weather. Both wear a type of 'poncho' cloak, which passes under the belt only at the front. One cloak is fastened at the chest with a toggle. Both wear broad-brimmed hats decorated with a mixture of feathers more resilient to campaigning conditions than the favoured but more fragile ostrich plumes. The handgunner wears a large kriegsmesser (knife of war) at his waist. Sturdy marching shoes like these may have been more common than the illustrations would have us believe, and would not get lost in the mud. (Eli Tanner/J.R.)

side, the schweizerdolch became a true symbol of the emerging Confederacy, as the large number in the Historical Museum in Basel testifies. Also, it was very rare for them to carry double-handed swords, preferring simpler hand-and-a-halfs and *kreuz* or *schweizerdegen*, medium-length swords with simple cross-guards.

The Landsknechts and the birth of Switzer – land

Throughout this book, and for reasons that will become apparent below, the author has been careful not to use the term 'Swiss' for the period up to 1500, since there was no such place as Switzerland at this time. The cantons and city states from this area that had formed the defensive coalition known as the *Eidgenossenschaft* had effectively kept themselves separate from the Holy Roman Empire and Burgundy right up to the end of the 15th century and in so doing had built up an identity based on common achievements and goals. The people from these areas resolutely referred to themselves as *Eidgenossen* (Confederates) and this remained the case well into the 16th century. In the years between 1476 and 1499, the Confederates had been the most sought-after mercenaries in Europe, bringing unparalleled wealth to the region. With the emergence of the Landsknechts, competition loomed, and although thousands of Confederates were to serve Imperial warlords and even

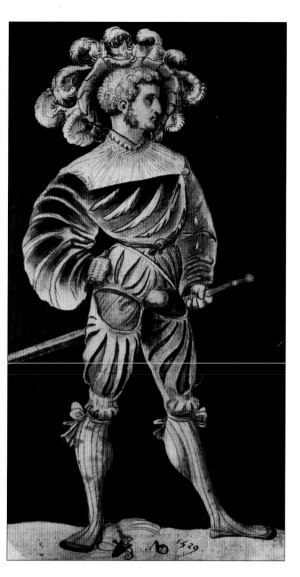

Reisläufer and Landsknecht, by Nicklaus Manuel Deutsch, 1529. A wonderful depiction of the classic stereotype Reisläufer and Landsknecht, confronting each other as they did in real life (see text). (Öffentliche Kunstsammlung, Basel)

OPPOSITE, BOTTOM *Landsknecht Halbardier*, by Paul Dolstein, c.1500. Dolstein's sketch depicts one of his comrades, Wihelm von Strasburg, wearing the St Andrew's cross of the Empire on breast and halbard. (Thür. Hauptstaatsarchiv, Weimar)

fight in Landsknecht units, discrete units of Landsknecht and Reisläufer would not easily mix and would view each other with suspicion.

At the Imperial Diet of Worms in 1495, Maximilian attempted to gain the approval of the states of the Holy Roman Empire for his Italian expansion plans. To pay for these, the states approved an Imperial tax, 'the common penny'. In return they were able to achieve a reform of the Empire. Since this effectively meant a strengthening of Imperial power, the Helvetic Confederation was naturally suspicious and extended a special agreement that had been signed with Bavaria in 1491 by entering a defensive alliance with France in 1495. Since Maximilian attempted to coerce the Helvetic Confederation into accepting the Imperial reforms by force of arms, tension mounted all along the frontier with increased skirmishing, until war finally broke out in 1499. The already bitter rivalry between Reisläufer and Landsknecht finally turned into armed conflict, amidst a veritable torrent of mutual abuse, insulting caricatures and mocking songs, made possible for the first time in history by the mass production of leaflets (the first example of true psychological warfare in the modern sense). The main insults were aimed at the farming tradition of the Confederacy. The terms *milchsüfer* (milk boozer), *milchstinker* (milk stinker), *chuefigger* (cow fucker) and *chueschnäggler* (cow cuddler) were common insults, while *chueschweizer* (cow swiss) became a general term of abuse meaning cow herd, country bumpkin or cow intimate. Gradually the name *schweizer* stuck, and the Germans increasingly referred to the Helvetic Confederacy as the *Schweizerland* (land of cow herds).

The first shots of the Swabian War were fired on 7 February 1499 when a small group of Imperial soldiers standing on the battlements of Gutenburg Castle saw a detachment of Reisläufer from the canton of Uri marching past on the other side of the Rhine. The Uri men were treated to shouts of 'moo, moo, plä, plä', whereupon they waded through the icy waters and set fire to a few houses in Mels (Imperial territory). A larger army at Feldkirch had to come to the rescue and drive the Uri men back across the Rhine. Not content, they followed on to Confederate territory but were bloodily repulsed a few days later with the loss of 200 men and two fähnlein. The Swabian War came to an end after a crushing defeat of a Landsknecht army at the hands of the Confederates at the battle of Dornach, on 22 July 1499. Earlier, Maximilian had commissioned Count Heinrich of Fürstenburg (1464–99) as a feldobrist and instructed him to raise an army. This army of 15,000 men then moved around Basel and laid siege to Dorneck

Landsknechts on a winter march. All of the arms and armour are originals, and the cloaks, costume and youth of the men are typical. Note that the camp follower in the foreground is wearing the Imperial peacock feather badge. (private collection)

Castle, near Dornach, about 8 km south of Basel. They must have felt secure, for the siege was much delayed by the pleasures of camp life, and the Landsknechts remained in front of Dorneck 'without a care, without a guard, with much amusement, games, singing, jumping and dancing'. Count Heinrich had received several warnings 'from many of the officers who, knowing the Confederate mode of war and having seen some on the Tschartenfluh, advised taking care and setting a watch while strengthening and fortifying the siege works, whereupon their Feldobrist in his long coat said that if they were frightened, they should go home.' The main body of the Confederate army arrived after a forced march lasting all night, and seeing the lack of preparation promptly attacked. Count Heinrich, who had been inspecting the siege artillery, was killed almost immediately. His troops, warned by the sounds of battle, managed to form a disordered line and gave a good account of themselves before the late arrival of the contingents from Lucerne and Zug finally decided the battle. Many Landsknechts were struck dead where they stood; those that did not manage to flee were run down and massacred. It is of interest to note that in the rout many Confederates were killed by their own side 'because of illegible field signs, none at all or just simple white ribbons, in the form of a cross,

The Horrors of War, by Urs Graf, 1521. Francisco Goya was not the first artist to attempt to show war in all its cruel reality. Urs Graf was an eyewitness to the terrible aftermath of battle. (Öffentliche Kunstsammlung, Basel)

attached to the hat and that soon fell off, or were knotted to the sleeve or to the hose'. The Landsknechts were shocked by the defeat and used propaganda to try to cushion the shame, accusing the Confederates of using a ruse of war: 'the Swiss are untrustworthy, they all wore red crosses, as if they were Austrians.'

A contemporary woodcut of the battle, published shortly afterwards as an official view of events, shows a few interesting details. Several vignettes have been particularly highlighted to prove to the observer that the Confederate victory was a heroic one. In the centre, Heinrich Rahn from Zurich is seen capturing the Strasburg banner. Closest to the observer is the figure of an ensign from Obersibenthal who has chased his enemy into the river and, having cut off his hand, is finishing him off with both his sword and his flagpole. On closer inspection, it becomes clear that the victim is dressed in the latest Landsknecht costume, with a slashed St Andrew's cross, peacock's feather and cut-off hose. The worst scenes of men being hacked to pieces have therefore been reserved for those figures that are clearly shown to be Landsknechts.

After the battle, an amusing incident gives us an insight into the mentality of the time:

> And good old Bitterle of Leimental, went around with a bodyguard wearing the silk shoes of the dead Count of Fürstenburg, decorated with a large white cross like a bishop's mitre. When asked by the Bishop of Worms whom he might be, he answered, 'we are the farmers who punish the nobility'.

Various songs were published celebrating the victory; an excerpt from the 'Dornecker Song' mocks the Landsknecht fondness for camp comforts:

> The Swabians came and set their kitchen up
> The cauldrons boiling all about
> But shortly after Vespers
> We cleared their kitchen out.

The victory at Dornach effectively ended Maximilian's hopes of keeping the Confederacy as part of the Empire, but the situation remained tense and the insults continued. Basel, on the front line, now had to decide where its future lay. There was a groundswell of opinion in favour of joining the Confederacy, but there was much tension in the city. One year after Dornach, an argument between two women about the theft of chickens ended up in the Basel schultheiss court. The accuser justified herself by explaining that the defendant and her husband were *Schwitzer*. 'You take what you find and you and your husband eat everything I have, because you are Swiss.' The defendant countered by saying 'that she was not a Swiss, but a Basler, and that her husband had marked their house not with three but only two Confederate crosses'. These were sensitive times and the term 'Swiss' was once again meant to be insulting. Gradually, however, like the 'Desert Rats' of the Second World War, the insulted took the insult as a trophy, along the lines of 'we may be Swiss, but we still beat you', and thus a country got a name.

THE LANDSKNECHTS IN THEIR OWN WORDS

Paul Dolstein

Paul Dolstein originally came from Torgau and was a bridge builder by trade. We are fortunate that he decided to keep a diary of his adventures at the start of the 16th century, and that it has survived. He seems to have carried out his occupation with many quite long interruptions, but always returned to it when unemployed as a Landsknecht. We first find him in the service of Duke Albrecht of Saxony, taking part at the siege of Montfort, in Holland, in 1491, where he was hit under the right arm by an arrow and badly wounded. He turns up again working as a master bridge builder on a project in Torgau, where he started work in 1496 'and continued until Sunday after St. Valentine's day 1498 and completed two piers'. In 1502 he was in southern Sweden and Norway with the army of King Hans of Denmark, where on 14 July he took part in the siege of Elfsborg.

> We were 1800 Germans, and we were attacked by 15,000 Swedish farmers (see illustration p.52 top). God gave us victory and we struck most of them dead. We were all wearing breast and back plates, skullcaps and arm defences, and they had crossbows and good pikes made from swords. Afterwards, the King of Denmark knighted us all and did us great honour and paid us well and let us return over the sea in 1503. I, Paul Dolstein was there and Sir Sigmund List was our Obrist.

He notes that the castle 'was made of wood and covered with turf. Every window had a gun'. Paul Dolstein took part in two small adventures in the Landshut War of Succession in 1504, received regular gifts of cloth from the tailoring department of the Saxon court in 1509, 1511 and 1513, before finally disappearing from the records.

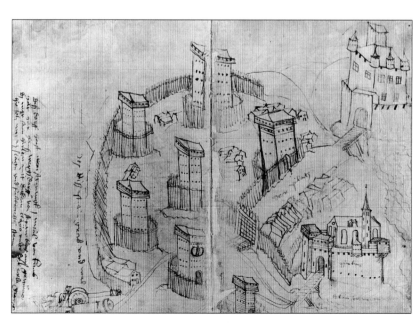

Siege of Montfort, **Holland, by Paul Dolstein, 1491. During the siege of Montfort in Holland, April to August 1491, Duke Albrecht of Saxony built a strong fortification depicted here in a rare eyewitness drawing by the Landsknecht Paul Dolstein. He depicts in detail artillery and siege equipment, the besiegers' stockade, gabions and earthworks, together with the outworks of the defenders. During the siege, the artist was wounded under the right arm by an arrow and later wrote, 'may one end in a braver fashion'. (Thür. Hauptstaatsarchiv, Weimar)**

Battle near Elfsborg, Norway, 1502, drawing by the diarist Paul Dolstein. Dolstein depicts his comrades under heavy attack from Swedish crossbowmen from Vastergotland, who wear a motley collection of old-fashioned helmets and their characteristic baggy trousers. Note that the crossbowman in the foreground wears a snapsack and canteen. The Landsknechts wear light armour and helmets. (Thür. Hauptstaatsarchiv, Weimar)

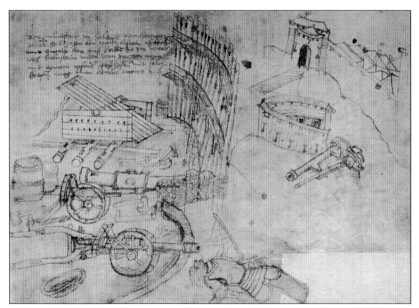

Fortified village, by Paul Dolstein, 1504. 'This village is Arnschwangk' wrote the Landsknecht artist, one mile from the small Bavarian city of Cham am Regen. The village, castle and church were heavily fortified, and wood and clay fortifications were built to take 23 serpentines and falconets. Mutually supporting tall blockhouses cover the outer ditch and wall. (Thür. Hauptstaatsarchiv, Weimar)

Niklaus Guldi

Niklaus Guldi was an excellent example of a certain type of mercenary, the type that joined up out of need and tried his hand at being a soldier without ever being particularly successful at it. He was the grandson of Hans Guldi, a glassblower who had moved to St Gallen from Constance in 1476. He trained as a cloth-shearer but was unable to find work. His involvement with the Anabaptists got him into trouble with the government of St Gallen, and he was thrown into prison and released on parole several times before finally, having broken the terms of his parole again, he was threatened with execution unless he renounced Anabaptism once and for all. He was banished from the city for one year but disappeared from the records for closer to four years before reappearing in St Gallen again in 1530, having spent time in Memmingen, Basel and Strasbourg, where 'he was unable to support himself because of inflation and the large number of poor people'.

In 1531 Guldi joined the St Gallen troops that went to support the men of Zurich in the Kappeler War. He served Captain Christian Fridbold as a personal messenger to the St. Gallen Council and seems to have managed to scrape a living this way, at least for the next few years. In the spring of 1535, while on a trip to Bozen, he allowed himself to be recruited for Charles V's expedition to Tunis. The Turks were always a serious threat to the Holy Roman Empire and had nearly captured Vienna in 1532, before being repulsed by Charles. In 1534 Barbarossa, the Turkish pirate much feared in the Mediterranean, crowned himself King of Algiers and Tunis. In the same year, he challenged Charles V by approaching Genoa with his fleet. The latter retaliated by raising an army of some 30,000 men and an armada of over 350 ships and galleys. Colonel Marx von Eberstein had been recruiting in the Meran and Bozen region and it was this Landsknecht regiment that Guldi joined. His experience as a messenger led him to prepare a very detailed account of the campaign that was sent to the St Gallen Council in the following year.

The account begins on 7 March 1535, when the regiment was mustered and marched to Peschiera on Lake Garda. It was here that the train of women and children were supposed to be sent back, but they took no notice and continued to follow the troops. The soldiers continued on until they arrived in the mountains near Spezia, where they were quartered in three small towns. After a five-day stay, they were again mustered in a field near Spezia and instructed on how food would be supplied while they were on the ships. Apparently, every soldier, whether 'big Hans or small Hans', was required to give one *batzen* per day to a central fund which would then be used to buy food in Sardinia or Sicily should the siege of Tunis take longer than expected and supplies ran short. Guldi complained later that none of these early agreements regarding food were kept and that they had almost died of hunger and thirst.

Landsknechts on the march. Landsknecht pikemen are shown trudging through the snow dressed for cold weather. The pikes used in this reconstruction are real ones borrowed from the castle at Grandson. The long shafts vibrated uncomfortably on the march and their length made them a nuisance to live with. They collided with branches overhead, making it difficult to follow narrow winding paths, and they could not be leant against anything low. You need plenty of space to lay them flat on the ground, especially when in a large group of men. It is little wonder that they are frequently shown carried on baggage carts. (private collection)

Two Landsknecht Musicians, by Paul Dolstein, c.1500. Many of Dolstein's drawings are remarkable because they are portraits of his comrades. Over each is written his name (sometimes sadly now illegible). We can, however, read that this drummer is Jan Fleming and the fifer Fritz von Wurmik. Both wear hats rather strange to our eyes, but perhaps we have become accustomed to the few images of Landsknechts that are well known. Both musicians appear to wear some sort of uniform livery. (Thür. Hauptstaatsarchiv, Weimar)

For they gave us 7 and 9 year-old bread that had been stored in Naples, which was also full of worms, spiders and moths; likewise the pork was in a similar condition, the water full of worms and stank like rotten meat; the beans were full of worms, the peas so hard that no one could be bothered to boil them, as no one would have eaten them anyway. Vinegar and oil, rice, fish and wine were good enough, but we only received food when the foreigners felt like giving it to us and not when it had been agreed.

The Landsknechts were loaded into 48 ships at Spezia, but remained in harbour for five days, and in this time Guldi and his comrades received their *sold*. While onboard, new rules applied. It was forbidden to carry weapons, let alone use them, and 'swearing and misuse of fire' were strictly forbidden. Law-breakers were taken by the *rumormeister* and whipped at the mast, or ducked in the sea. Serious cases were thrown into the sea or sent to do service at the oars of one of the many galleys.

At a rendezvous point off the island of Capri they rode at anchor for nearly a week until they were joined by Feldobrist del Vasto and approximately 10,000 Italian troops in 50 galleys. The combined fleet set sail for Naples, where they again dropped anchor. The troops were paid another *sold* (the last for five months) and were allowed to go on land. After loading the ships with provisions and heavy guns, the fleet set sail for Palermo on 17 May, where it again anchored for eight days before continuing to Sardinia and anchoring in front of Cagliari. On 12 June the Emperor arrived with his brother-in-law, the King of Portugal, in an enormous galley, the biggest in the fleet. By this time the fleet had grown to over 300 ships of 'flutes, galleons, galleys, half-galleys and polacres, with 100,000 soldiers and sailors'. The Emperor, who had bought more ships and troops with him, including the siege guns and 2,000 mounted men-at-arms, a galleon, four galleys of the Knights of Rhodes and six Papal galleys, was greeted by a salute from every one of the approximately 15,000 handguns in the fleet.

On 14 June the whole fleet set sail for Tunis and arrived in the harbour of Goletta the following day. The Emperor closed off Tunis harbour with 24 galleys and two galleons and then sent three galleys and two polacres against the fortifications of Goletta. As these ships moved in they came under heavy fire from a tower about half a mile from Goletta, and another three galleys were sent to return the fire. Having reconnoitred the harbour in this way, the Emperor gave instructions for the troops to disembark the following morning (16 June). Every soldier received food for three days (wine, cheese and bread) and was told not to drink from the wells, which had probably been poisoned. At dawn, the banners were unfurled and the troops disembarked to the sound of trumpets, kettle-drums, drums and fifes, whereupon the whole mass attacked in a disorderly and enthusiastic manner, the Spanish aiming for a high tower near the harbour and the Italians the tower that had fired the day before. The Landsknechts meanwhile stormed the nearest villages, which they promptly set on fire. Guldi describes in great detail the area in which he now found himself (which of course included the ruins of Carthage) and he noted that it was a very beautiful and fertile land, with fields of wheat, barley and hemp, which was spun into thread to make canvas. He felt, however, that 'it didn't appear to be much good, what they were spinning and weaving, but that our (St. Galler) canvas would be of great use in Barbary'.

Fortifications and artillery, c.1535, woodcut by Erhard Schön. Artillery positions with the guns set up behind earth-filled gabions were certainly in use as early as the 15th and until the end of the 19th century. In Landsknecht armies, the weaving and filling of gabions was carried out by the womenfolk and the boys. The Emperor Maximilian spent a considerable part of his budget on his artillery and all its supporting material. Justly proud, he had all of it recorded in beautifully illustrated inventories. The illustration shows a selection of beautifully cast bronze guns, the peak of advanced technology of the day. The big guns were immensely powerful; for example, in October 1523 King Henry VIII's gunner took only two hours to knock a hole 'as broad as a cart', in the walls of Bray, and in four volleys delivered from guns set up only 12 metres from the mighty fortifications of Montdidier, they bought down a great length of wall. Although the gunners were not Landsknechts, their clothing was clearly influenced by their gaudy comrades. (private collection/TMAG)

After five days the army started to move on Goletta, having waited for the heavy siege guns (over 100 pieces on wheels) and the horses to disembark. The Imperial tent was also erected and the whole camp 'stretched for over a German mile'. The army now proceeded to surround the fortifications of Goletta with earthworks, which were advanced every night. The fact that wood for supports and thousands of wine barrels to make gabions had to be brought in by ship meant that by the time the seventh trench had been completed, nearly a month had passed. While this work was being carried out, earthworks had also been thrown up all around the camp. The tower that lay half a mile from Goletta could not hold out for long, and once it had been captured the Emperor gave orders for his tent and those of the other princes and noblemen to be moved to this place.

A large wood of olive and fig trees stretched for about half a mile in front of Goletta, and the Turks used this cover to make daily sorties. The Landsknechts, who were camped closest to the wood, carried out an attack with half of the regiment and managed to capture three guns that had been firing from the cover of the trees. These guns, however, were immediately replaced by four more, which did so much damage that the Landsknechts finally received orders to take cover in the trenches. At one point the Turks attempted a sortie that made it right up to the Landsknecht trenches, without actually managing to break in. On the Spanish side the Turks were more successful and managed to penetrate the earthworks several times, thereby capturing two banners and a gun. In order to strengthen the Spanish positions, six fähnlein of Landsknechts (including Guldi) were detailed to reinforce the line. Guldi recounts having to keep guard in the trenches facing Goletta at night, while the sailors and the boys of the train threw up more earthworks and bastions for further guns.

On 12 July things were finally ready for the storming of the defences. Two hours before dawn, the Emperor and the King of Portugal arrived in the earthworks, ready for the trumpeters to sound the attack. At the same time, over 200 galleys had approached the fortifications from the sea and prepared their guns. At dawn, on a prearranged signal, the firing began. Each gunner was obliged to fire at least ten shots, and as the bombardment continued, four fähnlein of Landsknechts, approximately 15 fähnlein of Spanish and all the Italian troops mustered in the earthworks, prepared for the signal to attack. The Emperor ordered a barrel of Malvasier to be distributed to each fähnlein involved in the attack and the troops drank their fill; 'in this way we gained courage to fight'. The remaining men stayed with the guns positioned around the earthworks, ready to ward off any counter-attack. At 9 o'clock the signal was given for the attack and the storming of the defences took about two hours. The storming of a fortified position was always considered the toughest task of any on the battlefield, and often a *sturmgeld* (storming bonus) was paid to the troops who took part in this hazardous task. Despite the strong defences, Goletta fell and the Imperial troops were able to capture over 200 guns and approximately 30 galleys that had been stored inside. In the dungeons the troops found over 1,200 Christian prisoners, mostly Europeans, who were released and sent home. The Turks had, however, mined many parts of the fortification by digging large pits filled with gunpowder and some of these booby traps ignited, burning many of the advancing soldiers.

Having fortified Goletta, the Emperor sent an ultimatum to the city of Tunis, demanding that Barbarossa 'and two wealthy Jews' be handed over and that the city accept the Emperor as its sovereign lord. The city refused, explaining that it was under the control of a foreign Turkish army, whereupon the Emperor gave the orders for the whole army to decamp and move on the city with its siege artillery. According to Guldi, as the troops advanced on 20 July, the Turks attacked with approximately 30,000 men and fired their guns at close range. Guldi notes that most of the shots went overhead, while the return volley from the Imperial troops caused such slaughter that the Turks began to flee with the Landsknechts hot on their heels. Part of the Turkish force, however, feinted left and fell upon the train, which had been left behind unprotected at a well. A large number of sick soldiers, as well as women and children, were killed before the army, seeing what was happening, returned and drove the attackers off.

The Dance of Death. Death was the Landsknecht's constant companion and the Dance of Death was a popular motif. In an age when death was visible and frequent, people were not so squeamish and cut off from reality. There was much black humour and contemporary artists, writers and the Church used the close proximity of death to emphasise lessons in morality. (private collection)

As the advance on Tunis was renewed, Guldi notes that, 'it was so hot that the armoured men nearly suffocated and thought they would die of the heat, and when one went to help the other by loosening the armour, he would burn his fingers on the metal.' As the troops came out of the cover of the woods around Tunis, they were met by a hail of shot from prepared Turkish positions, and the Landsknechts were under fire for over three hours before their arquebusiers were finally able to force the Turks back. As evening approached, the Emperor arrived in 'a costume covered in gold and a beautifully decorated foot armour' and gave the order to set up camp in the woods. That night Guldi's captain, Baron Hans Markolt of Königsegg, and his Fähnlein, were set to do guard duty, and Guldi sat under the branches of the olive trees, looking at the stars and no doubt feeling nervous about the days ahead.

The next morning, the Emperor assembled all the Landsknechts, and after thanking them for their efforts up to that point, asked them not to plunder the city should they be successful in capturing it, as he wanted to win the hearts of the inhabitants. He pointed out that he was going to ask the Spanish and Italian troops the same thing, but this request cannot have been particularly popular, and in the event it was completely ignored. The Landsknechts now formed their order of battle and marched on Tunis, but not before they had left two fähnlein behind to guard the train. As the gevierthaufen approached the walls of the city, two noblemen rode out from one of the city gates and asked for the Emperor. They explained that approximately 10,000 Christian prisoners had been held in the citadel in the centre of the city and had managed to free themselves. When Barbarossa had arrived back in the city the night before, with the intention of killing all the prisoners and then escaping with his troops and all their plunder, he found the gates of the citadel locked against him and held by a determined group of armed prisoners. As the situation looked pretty hopeless, Barbarossa was forced to leave the city without carrying out his threat. On hearing this, the Emperor gave the order for the whole army to advance rapidly and capture Tunis before the Turks changed their minds.

Four fähnlein of the Landsknechts were the first to arrive at the gates and enter the city, while the Italians and Spanish used their pikes to climb the walls. The citizens of Tunis made the mistake of resisting the entry of the Landsknechts and a fierce fight developed in the narrow streets and on the rooftops of the city. The Landsknechts got into severe trouble as they were bombarded from the roofs with stones, boiling water and iron spikes, and had

Götz von Berlichingen, immortalised in this effigy from his tomb, von Berchlingen was the archetypal Landsknecht officer. (TMAG)

the other troops not arrived they would have had to retreat, leaving 'many proud men dead in the streets, as God knows all too well'. The attack had lasted three hours. As the citizens were forced back, the Imperial troops started to plunder in earnest, killing anybody that fell into their hands. Guldi notes somewhat sulkily that the Landsknechts were told to remain with their banners, as the Spanish and Italian troops could not be trusted. In the end, the Landsknechts were only able to plunder the houses in which they were quartered, but the pickings were thin because the other troops had already commenced plundering while the Landsknechts were still fighting.

Every man, woman and child that fell into the hands of the Imperial troops in the first two days was massacred, but as the fury passed, prisoners were taken and sold into slavery. Again Guldi notes that the Landsknechts played little part in this. The next morning, Guldi walked around the town in the hope of finding something worth carrying off, but had little success. In one house he found a popular edifying book in Latin called *Hortulus Animae* (the Garden of the Soul), but little else. However, the troops found plenty of food: 'in all the houses we found much barley and wheat, while a building near the Royal Palace was filled to the roof with good white bread. Here also was a fountain with sweet water, elsewhere there are only cisterns, and the mills are not driven by water but by donkeys.' Most of the loot, 'pearls, precious stones, velvet, silk, gold jewellery, cotton and sandlewood', was carried off by the Italians and Spanish. Even the corn sacks were so heavy that only the sailors and their labourers could carry them (presumably they were the only ones with lifting tackle). The Landsknechts came away with very little, 'apart from a Captain from Wangen, who found the silver service of the Prince'.

The air in the streets stank so badly from the corpses that lay everywhere that the army had to clear the city after eight days and then returned to the old camp near Goletta. After reinforcing the fortifications and leaving a garrison of 5,000 Spanish, the army embarked again and the Landsknechts set sail for Trapani, where they met the Emperor. To their fury, instead of receiving sturmgeld bonuses as they had been promised, ten guilders was docked from their pay 'for vittles on the ships and in enemy territory'. During their recruitment the Landsknechts had been promised that they would be fed and returned to Italian soil while in the pay of the Emperor, so Guldi calculated that by the end he was still owed 21 guilders, a tidy sum in those days. At least they got free passage back to Livorno and arrived there in September. From there they marched to Parma, losing many en route due to sickness, before the regiment split up, with some heading for Trient and others (including Guldi) returning to Milan.

By November, Guldi had arrived back in Chur, from where he dispatched his detailed report to

On the March, by Paul Dolstein, c.1500. Dolstein depicts the only named woman in his illustrations, Else von Win, marching along with a sturdy Landsknecht halbardier and a *trossbube* (boy of the baggage train), who carries a pewter field flask and is led by a small dog with bells on his collar. Else carries her baggage on her head, has hitched up her skirts over her hip belt and wears the black shoes with white leather tops frequently worn by Confederate and southern German women at this time. (Thür. Hauptstaatsarchiv, Weimar)

the council at St Gallen. He calculated that of the 7,000 men that had embarked at Spezia, only 2,000 had returned, the rest lost to sickness, wounds and accidents (700 German men, women and children were lost at sea in a storm on the way home). Guldi did not return to St Gallen until 1537, suffering badly from scabies and having lost what loot and money he had gained on campaign in various disastrous business ventures in Strasburg. In St Gallen, he promptly contracted a fever and had his horse (which actually belonged to his brother-in-law) impounded until he was able to pay a debt of one guilder that he owed to *Daughter Krutimhafens.* Deeply disappointed, Guldi left St Gallen to work as a schoolteacher in Otmarsingen, near Berne. His last letter to his mentor, Vadian, complains of the desperate straits he was in 'because of the war' and asks him 'should he be let go from Otmarsingen after "Fastnacht", to let him know if a suitable job should arise that would allow him to return and pay his fines and three years' taxes that he still owed.'

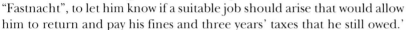

The Iron Biter. Woodcut, c.1512.
I am the Iron Biter,
known far and wide as a fighter.
Land and people I have overcome,
and did most of it with my tongue. (AP)

THE DECLINE OF THE LANDSKNECHTS

Over the years, the constant recruitment of men had brought many problems to the areas of Germany and 'Schweizerland'. Corruption, and the general lawlessness and sicknesses that the mercenaries had brought with them, together with the political destabilisation caused by large groups of men serving 'the highest bidder' led to a general disillusionment with mercenaries, and many cities, states and cantons forbade further recruitment. The fact that the basic Landsknecht *sold* of four guilders remained practically unchanged for nearly a century, while inflation whittled away at the value, shows the reduction in status of the Landsknechts.

The last meeting of Landsknechts and Confederates was on the battlefield of Ivry, 14 March 1590. For various reasons, 10,000 Confederate troops in the service of Henry V stood facing a regiment of Landsknechts and 6,000 Confederate troops in the service of the Catholic League. The battle was, however, decided by the cavalry before the infantry came to blows, and the army of the Catholic League left the field, leaving the regiment of Landsknechts and the regiment of Confederates lonely and forlorn in the centre of the battlefield. The Landsknechts surrendered and were murdered to a man. The Confederates, however, refused to capitulate, and were saved by the intervention of their fellows on the other side. They left with a certificate signed by the king that they had 'not surrendered nor laid their weapons down nor left their places in the Order of Battle, despite being cut off from all aid, until the King had offered them mercy, which under the laws of war, they were allowed to accept'. National solidarity had finally triumphed over mercenary thinking!

BIBLIOGRAPHY

Anderson, Christiane, *Urs Graf*, GS Verlag,
  Basel, 1978
Appelbaum, Stanley, *The Triumph of Maximilian I*,
  Dover Publications Inc., 1964
Bächtiger, Franz, *Andreaskreuz und Schweizerkreuz, zür
  Feindschaft zwischen Landsknechten und Eidgenossen*,
  Sonderdruck aus dem Jahrbuch des Bernischen
  Historischen Museum, 51 & 52, Jahrgang,
  1971 & 1972
Blau Friedrich, *Die Deutsche Landsknechte*, Starke
  Verlag, Görlitz, 1882
Dihle, Helene, & Adolf Closs, *Das Kriegstagebuch
  eines Deutschen Landsknechts um die Wende des 15.
  Jahrhunderts*, Zeitschrift für historische Waffen-
  und Kostümkunde, January 1929 (Band 3 (12))
Dihle, Helene, *Zur Belagerung von Elfsborg i. J.
  1502*, Berlin

Fiedler, Siegfried, *Kriegwesen und Kriegsführung im
  Zeitalter der Landsknechte*, Bernard & Graefe
  Verlag, 1985
Koegler Hans, *Urs Graf*, Urs-Graf-Verlag, Basel, 1947
Miller, Artur Maximilian, *Herr Jörg von Frundsberg*,
  Herder Verlag, 1933
Miller, Douglas, *The Landsknechts*, Osprey Publishing
  Ltd, 1976
Quaas Gerhard, *Das Handwerk der Landsknechte*,
  Biblio Verlag, 1997
Schiess, Traugott, *Drei St. Galler Reisläufer*,
  Neujahrsblatt für die St Gallische Jugend,
  St. Gallen, 1906
Treisssaurwein, Mark, *Der Weiss Kunig*, (illustrations
  by Hannsen Burkmair), Vienna, 1775
Von Mandach, C., *Niklaus Manuel Deutsch*,
  Urs-Graf-Verlag, Basel, 1947

COLOUR PLATE COMMENTARY

A: COSTUME

1. Shirt collars.
2. Front and back views of typical doublets. The point holes for the hose are visible along the waistline.
3. The three most important badges of the Landsknecht period. The Confederate Cross, the St Andrew's Cross of the Empire and the French Fleur-de-Lys.
4. Surviving shoes, modest in their design and made to stay on the feet.
5. Sometimes the hose was divided into short 'breeches' and 'stockings', joined together with points or laces. This is a detail rarely shown in contemporary illustrations.
6. The classic hose of the Landsknecht, with padded codpiece and slashed decoration, fastened to the doublet with points, i.e. short laces with metal tips rather like modern shoelaces.
7. Short ankle boots were occasionally worn, obviously more practical for marching, particularly in winter weather.
8. In Italy, as in other hot climates, various locally made sandals were worn.
9. A hypothetical reconstruction of Paul Dolstein, the Landsknecht artist, as he might have appeared while serving with an army employed by the King of Denmark in Vastergotland in 1502.
10. Rear view of a typical Reisläufer in 1515, wearing the red and white colours favoured by some cantons. Note the little bell on his ostrich feather.
11. In the 1490s and early 1500s, long hair might be gathered in a net shaped to fit inside the padded lining of a helmet.

***Two Halbardiers*, by Paul Dolstein, c.1500. These two serious gentlemen are clearly proud of the magnificent plumes that sprout from their hats. The man on the left has a curious whisker sprouting from his right cheek and a motto embroidered on the breast of his doublet. (Thür. Hauptstaatsarchiv, Weimar)**

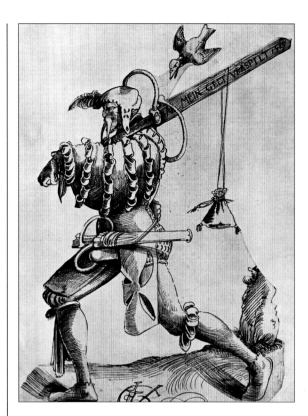

The Returning Landsknecht, by Urs Graf, 1519. Reisläufer Urs Graf cruelly caricatures his enemy, the Landsknecht, instantly recognisable by his costume, leather coif and weapons. The quillons of his swords are grossly exaggerated, his moustache bristles aggressively, and an empty purse dangles from his double-handed sword which bears the legend, 'I have gambled away my money'. (Öffentliche Kunstsammlung, Basel)

12. Civilian and soldier alike rarely went bareheaded, and close-fitting coifs were commonly worn. Some designs developed into more substantial hats, and one coif might be worn under a lighter one.

B: COSTUME

1. Coats like these with huge flat sleeves and a cloak-like body cut from almost a full circle of cloth could be extremely comfortable and large enough to wrap oneself in to sleep. The blue one shown here is a flimsier version with extravagantly slashed sleeves worn over a red and white doublet.
2. This 1518 self-portrait by the Basel artist Urs Graf shows himself as a Reisläufer and illustrates clearly just how large these coats could be, and how rakishly they could be worn.
3. A typical well-dressed Landsknecht in the more streamlined version of the costume from the 1530s.
4. Strong leather doublets with tasset-like projections were often worn by Landsknechts and could provide good protection against sword cuts.
5. A few examples from the bewildering variety of fashionable hats favoured by Landsknechts and Reisläufer alike.

C: ARMS AND ARMOUR

It is impossible to illustrate typical Landsknecht armour because styles changed, and old armours were kept in service alongside the latest fashions from Germany and Italy. Those who could afford armour wore it in battle but reluctantly on the march. How much looted armour was used is difficult to judge. Armour had to fit properly or it was more of a hindrance than a protection. Most armour was made up of a mixture of parts from different sources. In the armoury of the Churburg, the names of the solders that wore them are painted on the inside of each separate piece.

1. Half-harness for foot soldier made in Nuremberg, 1549, typical of the very efficient armour and open-faced helmets worn by the doppelsöldner in the front ranks.
2. A Maximilian armour of a style more commonly worn by horsemen. Interestingly, the picture shows the limit of upward movement achievable with the arms.
3. Foot soldiers generally wore a back and breast as illustrated or only the front half, held in place by leather straps crossing the wearer's back.
4. Infantry needed helmets that gave good protection but did not restrict all-round vision, and countless styles were worn. The top one is mid-15th century, the lower one is *c*.1510.
5. This Reisläufer, *c*.1525, wears fluted armour, an open-faced *sturmhaube* and a hand-and-a-half, or bastard, sword.
6. Schweizerdolch – These daggers became symbolic of the Helvetic Reisläufer.
7. Typical Landsknecht swords. Not all were as elaborate as this set, but a good sword was essential for survival and part of the 'ready-to-brawl' Landsknecht image.
8. A typical Landsknecht of the 1530s. Not very much different from his Swiss opponent.
9. Typical 'German' halbards. After a battle, captured halbards were not thrown away, so a variety of styles would usually be seen. Later historians, attempting to make order out of chaos,

Landsknecht and Swede, by Paul Dolstein, c.1500. The diarist Paul Dolstein records the peculiarities of the dress of his Swedish enemies, among which are the extremely baggy trousers (which could be rolled up when crossing mud flats), old-fashioned kettlehat and pointed shoes, long sword and unusual polearm. Dolstein notes that the Swedes had 'good ones made from swords', which accounts for the long blade and the curved crossbar. He carries a dufflebag snapsack and wooden-barrel canteen, items that have not appeared in any illustrations of the period to date. Both items are usually associated with soldiers of the 17th and 18th centuries. (Armemuseum, Stockholm)

imposed a rigid typology on polearm designs that would have been meaningless to the soldiers who carried them.

D: SIEGE OF TUNIS, 1535

Sieges were not the amateurish affairs portrayed by Hollywood. Large professional armies used all the technology of their age and considerable experience to reduce strong fortifications as swiftly and as thoroughly as possible. Tons of sophisticated equipment were transported or made on site. Specialised machinery: folding scaling ladders, jacks for prizing apart metal bars and grilles, explosive devices, winches, cranes, mines, etc, were widely used. In the foreground, a Confederate engineer in Landsknecht service, recognisable by his schweizerdolch, gives instructions to his colleages

E: *REISLÄUFER ON THE MARCH, MARIGNANO CAMPAIGN, 1515*

Attempts were made to control troops on the march, and discipline was usually strict, but pillaged farms and burnt homes always marked the passage of armies. Loot and the careful sharing of it had long been a particular concern of the Swiss cantons. Once clear of home territory, the Reisläufer and the Landsknechts took whatever they needed, often with great brutality. At the battle of Marignano, the Confederate Reisläufer were forced to retire from the battlefield with heavy losses. Little provision was made for the care of the wounded. Those that could keep up soldiered on, but badly wounded men were tended by the few surgeons that were available, and most of them were left to local charity or to die. The artist, Niklaus Manual Deutsch, is seen here riding in the column of Swiss, who show signs of the battle but also relief at having escaped unscathed. All the details in this picture are based on contemporary Swiss sources.

F: FRUNDSBERG RECRUITING LANDSKNECHTS FOR THE PAVIA CAMPAIGN OF 1525

The troops are shown drawn up in their ranks swearing allegiance to the Empire and to their feldobrist, Georg von Frundsberg, who is shown mounted next to the Imperial. At the table to their right are the administrative officers, the scribes and the pfennigmeister (master of the pennies). In the middle ground, the provost, who was responsible for the regulation of the market and discipline in the camp, sees off an enterprising shoe seller who has failed to pay his 'cut' (see text). Just behind them, pikes are shown bundled and loaded onto one of the hundreds of wagons. In the foreground, a cask of rotten meat has just been opened and the proviantmeister is arguing with a sudler. On the hill in the background, the commander's headquarters have been set up, protected by fortified battlewagons.

G: BAD WAR

Hand-to-hand fighting is relatively rare in modern warfare. In the 16th century, however, it was the Landsknecht's trade. Before battles, rival commanders would meet to agree terms of battle, in particular whether a 'good war' (quarter would be given, prisoners could be ransomed) or a 'bad war' (no prisoners, no quarter) was to be fought. When Landsknechts and their archrivals, the Reisläufer of the Helvetic Confederates, were on opposite sides, a bad war always

ensued. There can be few things that demand such raw courage as the clash of two bands of highly trained professionals armed with short swords and polearms. Experienced men would have developed their own individual and group tactics for dealing with the thick forest of pike staves and the tangle of whirling, stabbing blades and points. This picture attempts to capture the soldier's view of such a clash, but the reader should bear in mind the grimmer reality of a screaming, swearing, shouting mass, with men dying gory deaths on all sides.

H: TACTICS

It is clear from every source that the drill and training necessary to move Landsknecht formations had to be every bit as effective as that of Napoleonic units. Similar strategies applied and the well-trained unit would usually prevail. Here we illustrate a typical Landsknecht regiment coming into action, supported by a second coming up behind. The majority of the regiment's pikemen are formed in the classic *gevierthaufen*, a square whose flanks and front are protected by small companies of doppelsöldner handgunners, some of whom are breaking formation on the right front in order to go out as skirmishers. In the centre of the square are the banners, the musicians and the halbardiers. Two fähnlein, roughly a fifth of the regiment, have been dispatched to drive the enemy off the hill on the right flank. Their advance guard of handgunners can be seen going into action. The ridge in the foreground has just been cleared of the enemy's scouts by an advance party of handgunners on foot. Mounted crossbowmen have just come up to support them and are deploying to the left of the picture, while horse-holders guard their mounts. The obrist, the regiment's commander, followed by his bodyguard and staff, further supported by another company of mounted crossbowmen, is coming up the road to the right to see the situation for himself and direct the regiment's progress.

Battle, by Paul Dolstein, c.1500. Dolstein clearly depicts the favoured Landsknecht gevierthaufen, standing firm against charging armoured men-at-arms. The pikemen are all armoured, although none wear leg harnesses. The flank is strongly protected by arquebusiers while banners flutter bravely in the centre of the formation. One arquebusier can be seen ramming home a charge. The enemy horsemen appear to have some sort of field sign wrapped around the ends of their lances. (Thür. Hauptstaatsarchiv, Weimar)

INDEX